WHEN THE STARS CAME TO TOWN

Pop Package Tours at Derby's Gaumont Cinema 1959 to 1966

First published in the UK by Print2Demand in conjunction with
The Tap Publishing,
Suite 24, Parker House, Mansfield Road, Derby DE21 4SZ.
enquiries@thetap-publishing.com

ISBN number 978-1-910693-81-0

WHEN THE STARS CAME TO TOWN

Pop Package Tours at Derby's Gaumont Cinema 1959 to 1966

Roger Smith

PUBLISHING

This book is dedicated to my dear friend Eric Chapman whose wonderful collection of photographs inspired me to write this book.

Roger Smith

Contents

Introduction

The sixties are still regarded as the decade when pop music triggered a worldwide change in popular culture. When Skiffle groups evolved into beat groups and Britain ruled the air waves and the record industry. Led by the Beatles, the revolution swept our nation and the globe.

Well before the 'Mersey Beat' boom and the 'Swinging 60s' British teenagers could sense a change was coming and the demand to be part of this exciting new phenomenon wasn't lost on towns and cities like Derby. Teenagers weren't satisfied with seeing their pop idols in magazines, on the big screen or on TV. They wanted to see them 'live'.

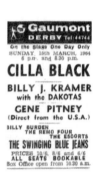

In the late 50s, switched-on entertainment entrepreneurs like Larry Parnes, Arthur Howes and Robert Stigwood recognised this and introduced 'The Package Tour'. These one-night shows which included several top recording artists and groups on one bill toured theatres and cinemas across Britain. Many shows presented two separate performances, or houses, and as many as seventeen nationally known stars on one bill. This of course limited the amount of time the acts spent on stage and some were lucky if they performed more than three or four numbers.

At first the tours were headlined by leading home-grown artists such as Cliff Richard, Adam Faith and Helen Shapiro but by the early 60s chart-topping American stars such as Roy Orbison, Gene Pitney and the Everly Brothers often topped the bill. At these shows the line-ups would include up-and-coming British artists, usually lower down on the bill. The tours proved to be the ideal platform for these bands and their members to promote themselves to British teenagers. It helped them climb to the top of the billings, sell more records and, in many cases, be elevated to global stardom themselves.

For example, one of the acts supporting the Everly Brothers, Little Richard and Bo Diddly at Derby's Gaumont cinema on 11th October 1963 was the Rolling Stones who were much lower down the bill and closed the first half of the show.

Unlike modern day concerts these package tours were usually hosted by a famous comedian or TV personality. The Derby Gaumont shows have seen the likes of Des O'Connor, Terry Scott, Norman Vaughan and Dave Allen take charge of proceedings.

Before the Gaumont presented its first ever package tour on 10th May 1959 other Derby venues had tried to get on the bandwagon. The Hippodrome Theatre on Green Lane was the first Derby venue to play host to the national pop package tours, though the line-up's tended to be smaller and more middle-of-the-road than rock and pop. On the 26th August 1957 the declining variety theatre presented 'Stanley Dale's National Skiffle Show and Contest'. This was followed by Terry Dene and the Dene Aces in September and Lonnie Donegan in November of the same year. The Hippodrome's first major tour saw Cliff Richard and The Drifters and Wee Willie Harris topping a bill which included an unknown singer who would later find international fame as record producer Micky Most.

Sadly these events couldn't save the theatre and on the 14th December 1958 it hosted its last concert which featured The Mudlarks, The Dallas Boys and Vince Taylor. The Hippodrome closed on 31st January 1959 after a seasons run of the pantomime 'Queen of Hearts' starring Jimmy Paige. The 'Hippo', as it was popularly known, stood empty for three years until it was purchased by Mecca and converted into a bingo club which lasted until 2007 when the theatre's doors were closed for good.

Despite a number of fires and partial demolition the building still stands and has been the subject of a long-running campaign by the Restoration Trust (DHRT) to secure and rebuild the theatre.

Other Derby venues were quick to take advantage of the demise of the Hippodrome as the main venue for national pop package tours. Later in 1959 the Majestic cinema in Wiltshire Road, Chaddesden, staged the first comeback concert of 'bad boy' rocker Terry Dene following his discharge from National Service on medical grounds. However, Dene, who had been hailed as 'The British Elvis', didn't ingratiate himself with the Derby public and the Evening Telegraph received scores of letters suggesting that he should "get his hair cut, do his duty and forget about his guitar strumming until he had completed his time in khaki".

Local entrepreneur Sammy Ramsden, who owned the Trocodero Ballroom on Normanton Road, Derby, also tried to fill the void and join the pop package tour revolution. However, these events usually featured a single headline act with local groups in support. He famously presented a show featuring USA rocker Gene Vincent in February 1961 but eventually gave up the ghost and Sammy Ramsden sold the Trocodero when he retired in 1964. This ballroom also eventually burnt down and was demolished, although the name lives on in a housing development on the original site named Trocodero Court.

Other smaller venues helped to satisfy the demands of the Derby teenager. Charting acts appeared at Mecca's Locarno ballroom, the Co-op Central Hall, the Rialto on Nightingale Road, and the Black Cat Club at Queen Street Baths.

However, it wasn't just the cinemas and large ballrooms that monopolised the scene. In 1964 the Corporation Hotel in Derby's old cattle market area, famous for its Trad Jazz nights, added a Friday Blues session to its programme. The following couple of years saw the likes of Rod Stewart, Long John Baldry, The Pretty Things and The Moody Blues perform on its tiny stage.

As the pop package tours gathered momentum and swept the nation the Gaumont cinema on London Road proved to be the only venue big and brave enough - and still in business - to bring these events to Derby.

In the seven years from 1959 to 1966 the Gaumont presented over 40 national pop package shows and provided Derby's 'Baby Boomer' generation with the opportunity to see national and international stars in the flesh. And, for the more avid gathering of fans that camped outside the rear stage doors on Osmaston Road, the chance to talk to, and even touch, their idols.

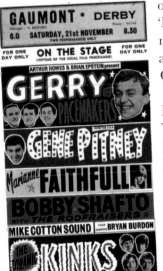

Besides The Rolling Stones, The Everly Brothers, Cliff Richard & The Shadows and Little Richard, the big names that took to the Gaumont's stage during that period included Roy Orbison, Gene Pitney, Cilla Black, The Kinks and The Who.

By the mid-sixties British teenagers were slowly turning their backs on live pop concerts in favour of discotheques and out-of-town 'all-nighter' soul clubs where they could dance to discs by their favourite artists.

The pop package tours dwindled and the last such event at Derby's Gaumont cinema, or as it was called by then, the Odeon, was on 23rd October 1966. When the curtain came down on the Walker Brothers it brought to an end a magical era in the history of Derby's popular culture. The theatre did continue to stage the odd pop concert after that but these usually featured single artists with Cliff Richard and The Shadows being the most regular visitors.

Besides doing my best to accurately chronical the famous names that have graced the stage of Derby's largest cinema, and share the memories of people who were in the audience, this book also presents a fascinating collection of photographs of 60s pop stars taken while they were in the city. Most of these shots were captured by Derby-born photographer Eric Chapman and their authenticity is proven by the distinctive retro wallpaper and curtains in the Gaumont's dressing rooms - a pictorial signature linking some of the world's most famous stars to Derby.

Chapter 1

1959 The birth of the Pop Package Tour

10th May 1959

Cliff Richard and The Drifters

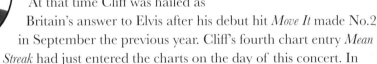

The first recorded Pop Package Tour concert at Derby's Gaumont cinema was headlined by Cliff Richard and his backing group The Drifters (later to become the Shadows). At that time Cliff was hailed as Britain's answer to Elvis after his debut hit *Move It* made No.2 in September the previous year. Cliff's fourth chart entry *Mean Streak* had just entered the charts on the day of this concert. In support were The Five Dallas Boys and dancer, comedian and pantomime star, Billy Dainty. Both were TV regulars in the 50s and the Dallas Boys were later described as "Britain's first boy band". The show was compèred by Tony Marsh. This wasn't Cliff's first Derby performance having appeared along with The Drifters at the Hippodrome in November 1958.

No.1 ON THIS DAY
ELVIS PRESLEY
A Fool Such As I

PROMOTER: Arthur Howes
CLIFF RICHARD & THE DRIFTERS
FIVE DALLAS BOYS
BILLY DAINTY
KAY & KIMBERLEY
TWO REXANOS
LESTER SHARPE & IRIS
RON SCOTT
TONY MARSH (COMPÈRE)

THE CLIFF RICHARD SHOW

Souvenir Programme

27th September 1959

Cliff Richard & The Drifters

| PROMOTER: |
| John Smith |
| **CLIFF RICHARD & THE DRIFTERS** |
| AL SAXON |
| PETER ELLIOT |
| THE JONES BOYS |
| ROY YOUNG |

No.1 ON THIS DAY
CRAIG DOUGLAS
Only Sixteen

Less than five months after their first appearance at the Gaumont, Cliff Richard & The Drifters returned when Cliff's first No.1 hit *Living Doll* was still in the charts. This was the last Derby performance by The Drifters before they changed their name to The Shadows to distinguish between the American Drifters who were Clyde McPhatter's vocal backing group. Soon after that they would find international fame themselves. The UK Drifters first appearance was in 1958 when they backed Cliff at his first large-scale appearance just eight miles up the road from Derby at the Regal Ballroom, Ripley. In support at Cliff's second Gaumont concert was British singer Al Saxon who had enjoyed a minor hit with a cover of Sam Cook's *Only Sixteen* earlier that month.

GAUMONT : Derby

2nd HOUSE 8.30
SUNDAY
SEPTEMBER **27**
FRONT STALLS 7/6
K 15

No ticket exchanged nor money refunded
THIS PORTION TO BE RETAINED

ARTHUR HOWES presents

THE **CLIFF RICHARD SHOW**

Cliff loses Drifters, but gains Shadows!

CLIFF RICHARD has "lost" The Drifters! The name of his group, which was adopted long before Cliff became a recording artist, has been changed to The Shadows because of the clash in America with an established group called The Drifters.

13th December 1959

Lonnie Donegan

By 1959 the Skiffle craze which had swept Britain in the mid-50s was in swift decline. However, Lonnie Donegan, the artist who was behind its popularity managed to establish himself as an international star with record releases and TV appearances well into the 60s. He was also credited for influencing many future pop stars including The Beatles, Brian May, Roger Daltrey and Mark Knopfler. Donegan headlined this small bill soon after his seventeenth hit single *San Miguel* hit the charts. He was supported by country/folk duo, Miki and Griff, who were discovered by Donegan and managed two weeks in the charts in October that year with their single *Hold Back Tomorrow*. Compèring the show was comedian Des O'Connor who went on to become one of Britain's best loved and most versatile TV personalities with Top 10 hits of his own. However, it's unclear if he was allowed to sing that night. Lonnie Donegan's only other appearance at the Gaumont, Derby, was when he starred in Aladdin and His Wonderful Lamp which ran for 6 days from 11th January 1965.

No.1 ON THIS DAY
ADAM FAITH
What Do You Want

LONNIE DONEGAN
MIKI & GRIFF
DES O'CONNOR

I was there!

13th December 1959
John Burley
Chaddesden, Derby

I first learnt to love the Gaumont as a child in the 1940's when taken there by my mother on our once weekly treats to the 'flicks'. It became my favourite Derby picture palace – an ornate and magical place where young dreams were born. Later, in my teens, when I was working at the Coop bakery on Osmaston Road, a fellow workmate, Doug, and I worked in our spare time for a London company that produced black and white portrait photos of the pop stars of the day. We used to turn up at the 'live' venues run by British Gaumont cinemas in Nottingham, Sheffield, Birmingham and, of course, good old Derby. There were normally lines of people outside waiting for admission. We would stroll up and down shouting "souvenir photos at half-a-crown". After shows we were often allowed back stage to meet some of the stars and on this day, Doug and I joined a drinks party that Lonnie Donegan was throwing in his dressing room. The guests were mainly female fans but besides paying lots of attention to his devotees he was also interested in the American-style lariat tie which I was wearing and wanted to know where I'd got if from.

Chapter 2

1960

Skiffle and Rock'n'Roll give way to Rhythm and Beat Groups

17th January 1960

Craig Douglas and Adam Faith

PROMOTER:
John Smith

CRAIG DOUGLAS
Special guest
ADAM FAITH
* * * * * * * * * * * * * * * * *
THE FIVE DALLAS BOYS
CHRIS WILLIAMS & HIS MONSTERS
* * * * * * * * * * * * * * * * *
THE JOHN BARRY SEVEN
* * * * * * * * * * * * * * * * *
DICKIE RICHARDS (COMPÈRE)

British singer Craig Douglas shot to fame when his cover of Sam Cooke's *Only Sixteen* topped the UK charts in 1959. He headed the first package tour of the 60s at the Gaumont during the week that his Top 10 hit *Pretty Blue Eyes* entered the charts. The show really had two headliners with Adam Faith being billed as Craig's special guest star. Faith's No.1 smash *What Do You Want* was still in the charts and his follow-up chart topper *Poor Me* entered the listings the same week as his Derby performance. The Five Dallas Boys made a return appearance and the backing band for the show was The John Barry Seven which found chart success later that year with *Hit and Miss*, TVs Juke Box Jury theme, and a cover of The Ventures *Walk Don't Run*. John Barry went on to become one of the film industry's leading composer/conductors responsible for the scores for eleven James Bond films.

No.1 ON THIS DAY
EMILE FORD
What Do You Want To Make Those Eyes At Me For

THE FIVE DALLAS BOYS

FAN CLUB
38 GILLIE LANE
RACECOURSE EST
HOUGHTON-LE-SPRING
CO. DURHAM

Russ Conway

Pop music pianist Russ Conway had a string of hits and two No.1s in the 50s and was a regular TV show guest. He was best known for his chart topper *Side Saddle* and his alluring smile but by the time he appeared at the Gaumont his popularity had begun to wane. However, he still maintained a loyal following amongst the older audiences and at the time of this show his recording of *Royal Event*, a tribute to the forthcoming marriage of Princess Margaret and Anthony Armstrong-Jones, was in the charts. The support cast included Bert (Play in a Day) Weedon who inspired many aspiring British guitarist and whose *Big Beat Boogie* was in the charts on that day. The compère for the evening was up-and-coming comedian Terry Scott who starred in many of the Carry On films and became a household name in the 60s and 70s when he partnered June Whitfield in the long-running 60s TV sit-com Terry and June.

RUSS CONWAY

EDDIE FALCON

BERT WEEDON

THE DEBBIE SISTERS

ROSA GOLDI

THE KEY SISTERS & KENNY

PETER CRAWFORD TRIO

TERRY SCOTT (COMPÈRE)

No.1 ON THIS DAY
LONNIE DONEGAN
My Old Man's A Dustman

12th April 1960

The Everly Brothers

No.1 ON THIS DAY
LONNIE DONEGAN
My Old Man's A Dustman

This was The Everly Brothers second major UK tour after supporting Buddy Holly and The Crickets in 1958, and the first time major American stars had visited the Gaumont. The event generated intense excitement amongst local teenagers as the Everley's No.1 *Cathy's Clown* had just entered the charts. After over a dozen hits in the 50s on the London label the duo moved to Warner Brothers and *Cathy's Clown* was the very first 45rpm release on this new UK label. Also on the bill were Lance Fortune whose Top 10 hit *Be Mine* was still in the charts, Danny Hunter and The Freddy Lloyd Five. The ubiquitous Dallas Boys also took to the stage for their third Derby performance in less than a year.

PROMOTER:
Arthur Howes

THE EVERLY BROTHERS

LANCE FORTUNE

FIVE DALLAS BOYS

CHERRY WAINER & DON STORER

DANNY HUNTER

FREDDY LLOYD FIVE

TONY MARSH (COMPÈRE)

I was there!

12th April 1960
Derby Evening Telegraph
W.G.

Voices in harmony on the stage v. voices in adulation in the audience produced a close finish at the Gaumont Theatre last night. It was much to the credit of the packed and youthful house, however, that they reserved their greatest applause for the more musical – and not necessarily noisier – artists. Top of the list in this category were, of course, the Everly Brothers, and even the most cynical member of the audience could not fail to concede that this delightfully harmonious, boyish enthusiastic duo enjoy deserved success. Following closely behind them in both artistic quality and audience esteem, the Dallas Boys proved themselves to be five young men capable of combining close harmony and genuine comedy. Although the application of the organ could scarcely have been foreseen by Bach, the warm applause that greeted the efforts of Cherry Wainer was no more than her deserts. Lance Fortune and Danny Hunter, two vocalists who clutched the microphone as if it was their last remaining friend, kept up the noise quotient and 'The Frantic' Freddy Lloyd Four did nothing to belie their self-styled prefix.

1st May 1960

Cliff Richard & The Shadows

PROMOTER: Arthur Howes
CLIFF RICHARD & THE SHADOWS
✶✶✶✶✶✶✶✶✶✶✶✶✶✶✶✶✶✶✶✶
JERRY LORDAN
✶✶✶✶✶✶✶✶✶✶✶✶✶✶✶✶✶✶✶✶
PETER ELLIOTT
✶✶✶✶✶✶✶✶✶✶✶✶✶✶✶✶✶✶✶✶
THE FOUR JONES BOYS
✶✶✶✶✶✶✶✶✶✶✶✶✶✶✶✶✶✶✶✶
KATHY KIRBY
✶✶✶✶✶✶✶✶✶✶✶✶✶✶✶✶✶✶✶✶
BILLY WOODS FIVE
✶✶✶✶✶✶✶✶✶✶✶✶✶✶✶✶✶✶✶✶
NORMAN VAUGHAN (COMPÈRE)

Cliff returns to the Gaumont for the third time in 12 months but this time billed as Cliff Richard & The Shadows. His backing band had changed its name from The Drifters in October the previous year.

No.1 ON THIS DAY
THE EVERLY BROTHERS
Cathy's Clown

Cliff's chart topper *Fall in Love With You* was still in the charts and his follow-up *Voice In The Wilderness* entered the listings that week. The bill included an early performance from glamorous English singer, Kathy Kirby, reportedly the highest-paid female singer of her generation. She went on to have chart success later in the 60s including her cover version of Doris Day's *Secret Love*. The show also featured a rare solo performance from revered composer/songwriter Jerry Lordon who had a hit earlier that year with his *Who Could Be Bluer.* Lordon is best known for writing the instrumental *Apache* which topped the charts for The Shadows later that year. The compère that evening was relatively unknown comedian Norman Vaughan who later found fame as a regular TV variety and game show host. The Derby date for this sell-out tour included excitement off stage too when Cliff's car was stolen whilst the entire cast were staying overnight at the White Horse Hotel in the Morledge.

I was there!

1st May 1959
**Christine Hardy (nee Blore)
Oakwood, Derby**

In the early 60s I worked in the cosmetic department of the Derby Coop in Albert Street, Derby. On fine summer days the shop girls would spend their lunchtimes on the roof behind the famous Coop Cow neon sign. The neighbouring building was the old Derby Evening Telegraph with its distinctive green domed roof around which the newspaper's staff would also gather. One lunchtime a guy shouted over to us Coop girls "Anyone like Cliff Richard?" I was an avid fan and quickly shouted "yes, me!". The guy shouted back: "Well meet me on the Spot at 7 o'clock and I'll take you into the show, but you'll have to carry my camera bag". It turned out he was one of the paper's photographers. That night I was taken in through the stage door posing as the photographer's assistant and I watched the show from the wings. It was so exciting. Cliff didn't travel on the tour bus and was driven to Derby in his white Sunbeam Alpine sports car by his driver/personal assistant who chatted me up behind the scenes during the show. The entire cast of the package show, including Cliff, were staying at the White Horse Hotel in the Morledge and after the show Cliff's driver asked me if I would like to wave Cliff and all the stars off in the morning. He picked me up from home at 5.30am and dropped me at the White Horse before going to get all the lipstick messages cleaned of Cliff's car. But the driver was never seen again and it was reported in the press that Cliff's car had been stolen. It transpired that the driver drove straight from Derby up to Scotland to visit his sick father. (That was his story anyway).

Cliff serenades Christine Blore (Centre) and her friend in his dressing room

CLIFF RICHARD HAS TRAVEL TROUBLE

THREE thousand Cliff Richard fans chanted "We want Cliff" at Bradford's Gaumont Theatre last Friday when the singer's scheduled first house appearance started almost two hours late—just as the second house seatholders were arriving for the concert!

Reason for the delay was that the coachdriver assigned to drive Cliff and other artists from Norwich to Bradford arrived three hours late at the picking-up point.

The second concert at Bradford did not begin until after 10 p.m.

Cliff's £1,000 sports car, which disappeared in Derby on Monday, was recovered over 300 miles away in Dundee the following day. In order to fulfil an engagement in Carlisle on Monday, Cliff chartered a special plane for the journey.

18th May 1960

Conway Twitty

PROMOTERS:
Don Arden and
The Eckart Bros

CONWAY TWITTY

FREDDY CANNON

JOHNNY PRESTON

WEE WILLIE HARRIS

**CHRIS WAYNE
& THE ECHOES**

TONY CROMBIE

DON ARDEN (COMPÈRE)

Just a couple of weeks after the Cliff & The Shadows show the Gaumont saw an invasion of American stars. Headlining was Conway Twitty whose No.1 *It's Only Make Believe* enjoyed 15 weeks in the charts in 1958. His single *Is A Bluebird Blue* was released two months after this show but would only make No.43 in the UK charts. Supporting were two fellow US stars that had both had Top 10 hits that year - Freddy Cannon reached No.3 with *Way Down Yonder In New Orleans* and Johnny Preston hit the top spot with *Running Bear.* Preston's No.1 was quickly followed up with *Cradle Of Love* which reached second place and was still in the charts at the time of this show. Also on the bill was popular 50s rocker Wee Willie Harris who was known as 'Britain's wild man of Rock'n'Roll'. The promoter and compère for the show was Sharon Osbourne's father Don Arden who went on to become a leading music manager and agent.

No.1 ON THIS DAY
THE EVERLY BROTHERS
Cathy's Clown

16th October 1960

Emile Ford

Emile Ford was an energetic star in more ways than one. This event was part of a short tour of Sunday concerts billed as 'One Night Stands' while he was appearing in Monday to Saturday week long shows in major UK cities. Ford had enjoyed a massive No.1 hit with *What Do You Want To Make Those Eyes At Me For* earlier in the year. His 4th release *Them There Eyes* was heading towards the Top 20 at the time of his Derby performance but only managed 18th position. National advertising listed The Shadows as 'Guest Stars' but they didn't appear at this concert. In support were Derby group The Skyliners which included local lads Lennie Bull, Geoff Cook, Alan Jervis, Ray Gittens and twins Dennis and Cliff Sleigh. After The Skyliners had won a contest to find the best group in Derbyshire they approached the tour's promoter, Arthur Howes, who agreed to put them on the bill for Emile Ford's Derby concert. Their lead-singer Lennie Bull went on to front a group named Paul Newman and the Excaliburs which made several appearances on TVs Opportunity Knocks. Also in support were George Formby impersonator Alan Randall, 'Britain's hottest new beat chick' Patty Brook and vocal group The Wiseguys. The compère for the evening was TV comedian Norman Vaughan who was returning to Derby after being in charge of proceedings at a Cliff Richard concert earlier that year.

No.1 ON THIS DAY
ROY ORBISON
Only The Lonely

PROMOTER: Arthur Howes
EMILE FORD
ALAN RANDALL
PATTY BROOK AND THE DIAMONDS
THE SKYLINERS
THE WISEGUYS
BOBBY DEACON AND THE CRUISERS
NORMAN VAUGHAN (COMPÈRE)

ARTHUR HOWES
PRESENTS
THE STARS
on ONE NIGHT STANDS
EMILE FORD
AND ALL STAR SHOW
WORCESTER, Gaumont
Sun., Oct. 2nd   5.30 & 8 p.m.
GUEST STAR:
RICKY VALANCE
SHEFFIELD, Gaumont
Sun., Oct. 9th   5.30 & 8 p.m.
DERBY, Gaumont
Sun., Oct. 16th   6 & 8.30 p.m.
PETERBOROUGH, Embassy
Sun., Oct. 23rd
GUEST STARS:
THE SHADOWS
★

Norman Vaughan

19

Derby group The Skyliners which supported Emile Ford

I was there!

16th October 1960
Geoff Cook
Derby

During this time I played piano in local Derby group The Skyliners. We were probably the most successful local group of the early 60s and appeared at all major venues - the Locarno, Sammy Ramsden's Trocodero, the Rialto, the old Assembly Rooms, Albert Rooms, Hippodrome, the Majestic cinema and the Regal Ballroom at Ripley. We won the annual Derbyshire Groups contest which was held at the Locarno for two or three consecutive years. Our biggest gig ever was at the Gaumont cinema supporting Emile Ford who was the hero of our lead singer Lennie Bull. The compere was Norman Vaughan, fresh from the London Palladium, and to play in front of nearly 2,000 people in a vast cinema as part of a top line package show was an awesome feat at the time. We were included on the bill after our guitarist Dennis Sleigh and I approached the Gaumont manager and the tour promotor Arthur Howes and asked to be included on the show. After a hard sell this was achieved and Lennie sang his 'showpiece' number Lucky Old Sun with full encouragement from Emile Ford. A truly memorable occasion.

26th October 1960

Billy Fury

The largest national pop package tour ever to visit Derby came to the Gaumont on Wednesday 26th October 1960. Billed as 'The Rock 'n' Trad Spectacular - The New Noise of 1960' the show presented an amazing seventeen different acts. The tour promoter was Larry Parnes whose strategy was to give his artists names that supposedly reflected the image he wanted them to portray. Billy Fury and Joe Brown topped the bill and supporting acts included Johnny Gentle, Dave Sampson, Duffy Power, Tommy Bruce and a still relatively unknown Georgie Fame. Also in support were the Vernon Girls who at that stage were a 16-piece vocal group. Soon after their show they cut down to just five members and went on to have a hit with *Lover Please*. Another interesting performer that night was Jimmy Nicol who later found fame when he deputised for Ringo Starr on the Beatles tour of Australia. Significantly, this massive show was produced by Jack Good, the pioneering TV producer responsible for the ground breaking 50s TV pop programmes Six-Five Special and Oh Boy!

PROMOTER: Larry Parnes
PRODUCER: Jack Good
'The Rock 'n' Trad Spectacular
The New Noise of 1960'

BILLY FURY
JOE BROWN
TOMMY BRUCE
NELSON KEENE
DICKIE PRIDE
THE VERNONS GIRLS
PETER WYNNE
THE VISCOUNTS
DAVE SAMPSON
JOHNNY GENTLE
DUFFY POWER
GEORGIE FAME
BILLY RAYMOND
JOHNNY GOODE
RED PRICE
WITH JIMMY NICOL
THE VALENTINE GIRLS
THE DALE SISTERS

Rock 'n Trad Spectacular
THE NEW NOISE OF 1960
STARRING
Billy Fury AND HIS COMPANY OF 50
SOUVENIR PROGRAMME   ONE SHILLING

I was there!

26th October 1960
Clive Greatorex
Michigan, USA

I played bass guitar in one of the first Derby groups, Ken Barker and the Jets, along with some school friends from Central School, later known as Henry Cavendish School. I lived in Canal Street, Derby and when I was on my way to a gig downtown with my bass guitar I passed the Gaumont and saw the poster outside advertising the upcoming big show - The Rock'n'Trad Spectacular - and managed to get my photograph taken as I passed by. Although I didn't make it to that particular show I would always try to go to other Gaumont package tours whenever my own performance commitments allowed.

Clive Greatorex

Chapter 3

1961 The end of the road for 50s favourites

6th February 1961

Cliff Richard & The Shadows

PROMOTER: Arthur Howes
CLIFF RICHARD & THE SHADOWS
THE BROOK BROTHERS
CHAS McDEVITT & SHIRLEY DOUGLAS
THE HUNTERS
DAVE SAMPSON

By the time Cliff Richard headlined his fourth Gaumont concert The Shadows enjoyed equal billing and their third single *FBI* was about to enter the Top 20. Cliff's *I Love You* was still in the charts but on its way down, soon to be replaced by *Theme For A Dream* which went on to reach No.3. Supporting acts included The Brook Brothers who had just released *Warpaint* which would go on to make the Top 10 the following month. Uttoxeter born Dave Sampson, who had a minor hit with *Sweet Dreams* the previous year, made a return visit after having been part of Jack Good's 'Rock 'n' Trad' Spectacular three months earlier.

No.1 ON THIS DAY
ELVIS PRESLEY Are You Lonesome Tonight

CLIFF RICHARD
COLUMBIA RECORDS

I was there!

Neil Hallam
Belper, Derbyshire

As a 16-year-old trainee journalist on the Derby Evening Telegraph, my usual duties involved such intellectually challenging tasks as re-writing reports submitted by local Women's Institute, covering schoolboy football matches and reporting on minor cases at the magistrate's court. When I heard that Cliff Richard and the Shadows were to appear at the Gaumont, however, I saw more glamourous possibilities and suggested that this would make a great feature piece for the picture edition. The idea of aiming at young readers with front-page coverage of a pop concert was pretty revolutionary at that time but the editor gave the thumbs up and that show became the first of several at the Gaumont to get the big feature treatment. My status as the lowliest form of journalistic life meant that I was accompanied by two mildly bemused senior reporters. Bruce Welch of the Shadows answered my knock on the dressing room door and said "I suppose you're here to see the famous one." Cliff was polite, approachable and patient – a true gent. He didn't even get rattled when one of the senior hacks – Winchester and Oxford don't you know – baffled us all by asking whether he was a devotee of the "method acting school of Stanislavski and Lee Strasberg." I asked Cliff for his autograph for my sister, who claimed "He knocks spots off Elvis," and he obliged with a photo signed by him and all the Shadows. I interviewed many lesser known stars but I'd say Cliff was probably the most cooperative and the one with the smallest ego. That picture edition sold out in no time.

Shirley McGuiness (nee Miller)
Paignton, Devon

At the tender age of 15 while I was a pupil at Homelands School I was a 'mad' Cliff fan. That lasted for about three years until The Beatles changed everything and introduced me to original Blues and R&B. While I was still under Cliff's spell, and still at school, my dear mother queued outside the Gaumont cinema all morning to get me a ticket for his concert. On the morning of the show I was allowed to go into town and wait outside the stage door in the hope of getting the autograph of my heart-throb. I stood outside with other girls for hours clutching a copy of his LP 'Cliff Sings' in the hope that he'd sign it. He didn't show but I did manage to get the signatures of Bruce Welch and Tony Mehan so it wasn't all in vain, and the show itself was like a dream come true.

24th March 1961

Frankie Vaughan

Crooner Frankie Vaughan made his name in the mid-50s with his Top 10 hit *Green Door* and No.1 *Garden Of Eden.* His chart success continued well into the 60s due to a faithful middle-aged female following which had been wooed by his inimitable stage presence and his trademark tuxedo, top hat and cane. He was dubbed 'Mr Moonlight' after one of his early hits *Give Me The Moonlight.* Supporting acts for this performance including comedian Harry Worth who, along with his shop window mirror trick, went on to find TV fame. This was Frankie Vaughan's first and last Gaumont appearance although, in his role as president of the National Association of Boys' Clubs, he visited the newly formed Derby Merlin Boy's Club in May 1963.

No.1
ON THIS DAY
THE EVERLY BROTHERS
Walk Right Back

oto: *Derby Telegraph*

9th April 1961

Emile Ford & The Checkmates

PROMOTER:
Arthur Howes

EMILE FORD & THE CHECKMATES

BOBBY DEACON

PATTY BROOK AND THE DIAMONDS

FRANK IFIELD

THE FORDETTES

BOB & JACK

ALAN FIELD (COMPÈRE)

This was Emile Ford's second visit to the Gaumont having appeared at a 'one man show' the previous year. He got to No.4 with his hit *Counting Teardrops* four months earlier but didn't make the Top 20 again after

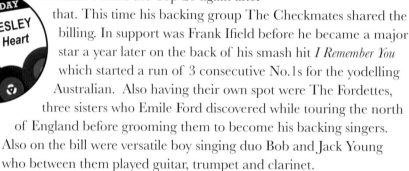

No.1 ON THIS DAY
ELVIS PRESLEY
Wooden Heart

that. This time his backing group The Checkmates shared the billing. In support was Frank Ifield before he became a major star a year later on the back of his smash hit *I Remember You* which started a run of 3 consecutive No.1s for the yodelling Australian. Also having their own spot were The Fordettes, three sisters who Emile Ford discovered while touring the north of England before grooming them to become his backing singers. Also on the bill were versatile boy singing duo Bob and Jack Young who between them played guitar, trumpet and clarinet.

20th April 1961

The Allisons

PROMOTER:
Joe Collins

THE ALLISONS

JOE COLLINS

RONNIE CARROLL

RHET STOLLER &
THE STRANGERS

THE KREW KATS

THE HUNTERS

MICHAEL HILL

DAVE SAMPSON

DAVE REID (COMPÈRE)

Topping the charts on this day with *Are You Sure* were The Allisons who had found fame earlier that year by being voted into second place when they represented The United Kingdom in the 1961 Eurovision Song Contest. This justified top billing on this tour which was supported by pop stalwart Ronnie Carroll who had earlier chart success with a string of American covers including *Footsteps*. Also in support was Dave Sampson, his third appearance on a Derby Gaumont bill in less than six months. Thanks to the Shadows who were responsible for a rapid rise in the popularity of guitar-based instrumentals at this time, the bill also included three groups which had enjoyed minor chart success - Rhet Stoller & The Strangers (*Chariot*), The Krew-Kats (*Trambone*) and Dave Sampson's backing group The Hunters (*Golden Earrings*).

No. 1
ON THIS DAY
THE ALLISONS
Are You Sure?

THE ALLISONS on **fontana** RECORDS

RONNIE CARROLL on
PHILIPS RECORDS

THE ALLISONS
"*Are You Sure*"
?
YES! 1st in London
2nd at Cannes

7th May 1961

Adam Faith

PROMOTER:
Joe Collins

ADAM FAITH
JOHN BARRY SEVEN
CHRIS CARLSEN
GERRY DORSEY
JOHNNY LE ROY
DAVE ALLEN (COMPÈRE)

Adam Faith had first appeared at the Gaumont in January 1960 when he was billed as the special guest star at the Craig Douglas concert. This time Faith topped the bill having had an impressive six Top 10 hits since then and his *Easy Going Me* was in the charts on that day. His supporting acts appear to be much more interesting than they were back then. Gerry Dorsey ended up equalling Faith's fame as Englebert Humperdinck and it was a return visit to Derby for the now legendary film theme composer John Barry whose group also provided backing that night. Another interesting name on the bill was the show's compère, Irishman Dave Allen, who went on to become one of TVs most popular comedians.

No.1 ON THIS DAY
THE TEMPERANCE SEVEN
You're Driving Me Crazy

I was there!

7th May 1961
Neil Hallam
Belper, Derbyshire

I was a junior reporter on the Derby Evening Telegraph when Adam Faith came to the Gaumont and wasn't quite sure what to expect when I was ushered in to see him. He had seven top ten hits and two number ones to his name so I thought he might be a 'Jack the lad' Cockney type but that wasn't the case. He was very modest and spent most of the interview being deprecating about his ability. I remember him saying "I'm no Mario Lanza. The only difference between you and me is that I am sitting here and you're sitting there. I was just in the right place at the right time". When I pointed out that he hadn't heard me sing he said "Well you can't possibly sing as badly as me." That prompted me to ask about his ambitions and he replied "To keep getting away with this for as long as possible and then I'd really like to get into acting." And of course he went on to have a successful career as an actor in film and television including the 70s TV series Budgie. As I left, he said: "Don't make me sound like a complete plonker" – the first time I had heard that term. The compère for this show was a then little-known Irish comedian Dave Allen and he didn't do badly for himself either.

I was there!

7th May 1961
Margaret Robinson
(nee Margaret 'Beti' Sturt)
Mickleover, Derby

This was my very first pop concert at the Gaumont and I was only 13. I went with my best friend and classmate Cherrylin Smith who, like me, was a 'mad' Adam Faith fan. Our parents made it very clear that we had to catch the bus home immediately after the show. I was so excited to be going to such a big event and even remember exactly what I was wearing that night; a pink mohair skirt and a gipsy blouse with a 4 inch wide, white belt. I felt really grown-up and despite wearing what were very trendy clothes at that time we decided not to put our make-up on so that we could get half-price on the bus. I travelled from Borrowash and Cherrylin joined me from her stop in Chaddesden but as soon as we got off at Derby bus station we dashed into the 'ladies' and applied our lipstick, make-up and eye-liner. The show itself was just as memorable and we were absolutely star struck. When Adam Faith came on stage everyone stood up and some ran, screaming, down to the front. This was all so new to us so we just did what the others did and joined the throng in the aisle. But we had to keep jumping up and down so that we could get a glimpse of our idol. The John Barry Seven were very professional and this was also the first time we had seen a proper band 'live' which even included violins. As we made our way out after the show we were 'on the ceiling' and heard someone shout that Adam was at the stage door. Without thinking we joined the other girls and ran round the corner to Osmaston Road. After waiting several minutes he didn't show up and we soon came back down to earth when we had to leave to get the bus home to meet our curfew deadline. This adventure started a run of over fifteen Gaumont concerts that Cherrylin and I would attend together but for me this one will always be the most memorable.

GAUMONT : Derby
ADAM FAITH SHOW
1st Performance at 6-0 p.m.
SUNDAY
MAY 7
FRONT STALLS 8/6
H15
No ticket exchanged nor money refunded
THIS PORTION TO BE RETAINED

7th May 1961
Brian Sims
Swarkestone, Derby

I met my future wife, Pauline, on a blind date on Friday 13th January 1961. We both lived in Borrowash and arranged to meet at Derby bus station. It turned out to be a lucky day for us because we haven't been apart since. On one of our early dates, when I was still trying to make a big impression, I took Pauline to the Gaumont in Derby to see our first ever pop concert which starred Adam Faith. It must have worked because after attending many other early 60s package tours together we finally tied the knot on another significant date, April 1st 1967, and we recently celebrated our Golden Wedding anniversary. We still have memorabilia from those magical shows but it wasn't until years later that we noticed that Adam Faith was supported by two stars in the making - Jerry Dorsey who later became Englebert Humperdinck and the compère on the night, comedian Dave Allen.

Englebert Humperdinck

10th November 1961

Russs Conway

This was the smiling, pop pianist's final appearance at The Gaumont and the last of the 'middle-of-the-road' shows. Russ Conway's Top 10 *Toy Balloons* charted a few weeks after this date but these 50s stars were slowly being muscled out by the new sound of the 60s. None of the other support acts that day had enjoyed UK chart success. However, Dusty Springfield started her career as a member of The Lana Sisters until, in 1960, she left to join her brother Tom to form The Springfields. The Lana Sisters only sniff at chart success was when in the previous year their *You Got What It Takes* made No.10 in Ireland.

No.1 ON THIS DAY
HELEN SHAPIRO
Walkin' Back To Happiness

The Lana Sisters

Chapter 4

1962 — Cliff & The Shadows still Derby's favourites

28th January 1962

Cliff Richard & The Shadows

PROMOTER:
Arthur Howes

CLIFF RICHARD & THE SHADOWS

DALLAS BOYS

PATTI BROOKS

THE TREBLETONES

THE TWO TONES

TONY MARSH (COMPÈRE)

Cliff and the Shadows were becoming Derby Gaumont regulars with their fifth appearance since their debut in May 1959. On this occasion Cliff was at No.1 in the charts with the title hit from his film *The Young Ones*. In support was Patti Brooks, not to be confused with the American singer Pattie Brooks. The British Patti sang duet with Cliff on *The First Lessons In Love* for The Young Ones soundtrack although leading lady Carol Gray mimed to her track in the film. Also on the bill were boy band The Dallas Boys, who were also becoming Gaumont regulars, and The Trebletones who made their name performing at Butlins Holiday Camps.

No.1
ON THIS DAY
CLIFF RICHARD
The Young Ones

Flowers... a love note... lie at his feet... Cliff stoops to gather a tribute as he sings a favourite ballad

Photo: Derby Telegraph

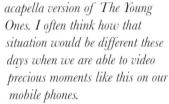

I was there!

**28th January 1962
Shirley McGuiness (nee Miller)
Paignton, Devon**

This was the second time that I saw Cliff at the Gaumont and, as I had the year earlier, I spent the morning of the show outside the stage door on Osmaston Road. There were a lot more girls with the same idea this time and whenever the stage door opened a collective scream would go up. Around lunchtime many of the girls had wandered off in disappointment at not seeing their idol, but I stuck around with about half a dozen other girls. Just as I was about to give up the ghost an anonymous man popped his head out of the door. One of the girls shouted "Can you ask Cliff to come out to see us?" He said no, because we'd scream and attract the attention of more girls and it would be mayhem. We promised faithfully not to scream and eventually, to our delight and excitement, Cliff came out and signed autographs including my book called 'Cliff Richard - It's Great to be Young'. He was so friendly and chatted with us for several minutes. Then, still stifling the urge to scream, one of the girls said something like "Give us a song Cliff" and he proceeded to render an acapella version of The Young Ones. I often think how that situation would be different these days when we are able to video precious moments like this on our mobile phones.

11th February 1962

Adam Faith

This show was something of a 'swan song' for the artists that had made their names in the 50s. It was Adam Faith's third appearance at Derby's Gaumont and each time he was backed by The John Barry Seven. On this day Faith's *Lonesome* was at No.16 but this release didn't make the top ten. However, it was in this year that John Barry wrote his iconic *James Bond Theme* which charted later that year. Also on the bill was British singer/songwriter and pianist Brad Newman who reached No.47 in the charts later that month with his own song *Somebody to Love*. Newman was resident on the 1959 BBC TV pop show Drumbeat which also featured Adam Faith and John Barry. Desmond Lane, another fading 50s performer, also took to the stage that night. He had enjoyed a brief spell of fame when he performed with the Cyril Stapleton Orchestra in the mid-50s.

No.1 ON THIS DAY

CLIFF RICHARD
The Young Ones

UMONT : Derby
DAM FAITH SHOW
1st Performance 6-0 p.m.
SUNDAY 11
FEBRUARY
RONT STALLS 8/6
F28
No ticket exchanged nor money refunded
THIS PORTION TO BE RETAINED

I was there!

11th February 1962
Cherrylin Stockley (nee Smith)
Hinckley, Leicestershire

At this time I was living in Chaddesden and, having experienced my first pop concert the previous year with my best friend Beti Sturt, we were so excited to hear that our idol, Adam Faith, would be returning to Derby. This time we weren't so naive and managed to get seats closer to the front in Row F. We had a much better view and I remember thinking how handsome Adam was in the flesh and the performance left us shouting and screaming for more. The previous year we didn't get to meet our heart-throb but this time we were determined. After the show we went round to the stage door to try again and joined about twenty girls who were all shouting his name. Eventually a man came out and to our delight announced that we could go in two at a time to meet Adam and get his autograph. Beti and I went in together and Adam was sitting at a table just smiling at us as we nervously approached. He immediately put us at ease and chatted to us for several minutes. But the conversation was a bit one-sided as we were too dumbstruck to say anything other than "yes" and "no". For saying he was a big star I'll never forget how friendly and relaxed he was, and so, so handsome. We eventually shuffled out and passed two other girls on their way in. As we walked away to catch our bus we were so excited by the experience of meeting our star, but at the same time so angry that we had acted like stupid little children and didn't make the most of the opportunity.

Billy Fury

PROMOTER: Larry Parnes 'The Big Star Show of 1962'
BILLY FURY
JOHN LEYTON
EDEN KANE
JOE BROWN
THE VISCOUNTS
RICKY STEVENS
KARL DENVER TRIO
SHANE FENTON
THE BLUE FLAMES
DON MUNDAY (COMPÈRE)

This period was the heyday for Pop Package Tours and was the third concert to visit Derby's Gaumont cinema in just over 3 weeks. Billed as 'The Big Star Show of 1962', it starred Billy Fury whose Top 10 *I'd Never Find Another You* was still in the charts. Fury was backed by another Larry Parnes act, The Blue Flames, which included Georgie Fame on keyboards. In support were other current charting acts The Karl Denver Trio (*Wimoweh*) and Eden Kane (*Forget Me Not*). Completing the impressive 'Big Star' line-up was Joe Brown, just before releasing his No.2 hit *Picture Of You* and other recent hit-makers John Leyton, and Shane Fenton with his Fentones. Other acts included vocal trio The Viscounts, one of which was Gordon Mills who later found great success as a songwriter and who wrote *It's Not Unusual* for Tom Jones. Also performing and supplying backing that night were Peter Jay & The Jaywalkers.

Billy Fury

I was there!

22nd February 1962
Kenny Barker
Blackpool

My best friend at Henry Cavendish School was Clive Greatorex and we both played for one of Derby's first beat groups. Our group, The Jets, sometimes played at the Mecca Locarno ballroom in town and the leader of its resident dance band, Ray McVay, liked what he heard. He wanted to introduce a more modern sound to his performances so that he could include the pop songs of the day into his repertoire, so he asked us both to play for his band whenever we were available. At that time I was a big Joe Brown and Cliff Richard fan and used to sing and play their numbers for the Ray McVay band. When I heard that Joe Brown was performing round the corner at the big Gaumont pop concert I managed to get a ticket for the early performance before my gig with the dance band. The show didn't disappoint and it featured most of the artists in the Larry Parnes stable with their distinctive stage names – Fury, Gentle, Pride, Fame, Power, etc. But I was really there to see my hero Joe Brown and I didn't have to wait long. Being a budding musician myself I always took an interest in the backing bands and during one of the performances by a lesser-known warm-up act I noticed that a guitarist in the backing band had a hat pulled right down over his eyes. It was Joe Brown and he was obviously trying not to pre-empt the excitement of his appearance higher up the bill. But I'm sure no one else in the audience would have noticed that though.

22nd February 1962
Clive Greatorex
Dexter, Michigan, USA

I was only 16-years-old and still at school when Ray McVay, the leader of the band at the Mecca Locarno Ballroom, invited Ken and I to play with his band. The dance bands of the day were finally beginning to accept that electric guitars were taking over from the traditional piano, double bass, drums and brass ensembles and the appearance of a couple of young local lads on teenage dance nights made sense. Ken and I played with the band on Sundays and Thursdays. It was after a Thursday night performance that I met Georgie Fame. He had been appearing at the Gaumont show and was playing in Billy Fury's backing group The Blue Flames. I went to the early show and remember Billy singing Wondrous Place and inserting a rather long pause before the last line of the song. After the show it was on to the Locarno to play with the band where, at the conclusion of our sets, Ken and I would often go to the coffee bar over the Locarno stage for a cup of coffee. It was there that I recognised Georgie sitting alone at a table. I asked if I could join him and after introducing myself he said "Clive? That's my name too." He was indeed Clive Powell, better known as Georgie Fame, the stage name given to him by the promoter Larry Parnes. I have since learnt that Billy Fury wasn't happy with the Blue Flames and fired them in favour of the Tornadoes at about this time. So that could well have happened on the night that I sat and talked with Georgie, but he went on to do better things anyway.

Helen Shapiro

PROMOTERS:
Bernard Hinchcliffe /
Arthur Howes

HELEN SHAPIRO
THE BROOK BROTHERS
THE FOUR JAYS
RED PRICE BAND
THE DALE SISTERS
COLIN DAY
DAVE ALLEN (COMPÈRE)

By the time 16-year-old Helen Shapiro made her debut on a Derby stage she had notched up an amazing four Top 10 hits in less than 12 months. Two of these, *You Don't Know* and *Walking Back To Happiness*, made the top spot and *Tell Me What He Said* was at No.2 on this day. The teen star was supported by The Brook Brothers who had appeared at The Gaumont in February 1961 when they supported Cliff Richard & The Shadows. Since then the duo had been unable to repeat their earlier chart successes and their latest release *He's Old Enough To Know Better* only managed one week at No.37. Hailing from Goole, Yorkshire, The Dale Sisters were also on the bill but the 'real' sisters only chart entry *My Sunday Baby* only managed No.36 the previous November. Making a return visit to compère the show was the still relatively unknown Irish comedian Dave Allen and a year after this appearance he left Britain and found fame in Australia. After a few years he returned to establish himself as a major TV star hosting his own shows which ran from the late 60s until the early 90s.

No.1
ON THIS DAY
THE SHADOWS
Wonderful Land

BROOKS BROTHERS
PYE RECORDS

Dave Allen

26th October 1962

Billy Fury

Although Billy Fury topped the bill, this concert was simply promoted as 'The Mammoth Star Show of 1962'. It featured 8 British acts that had all enjoyed recent Top 20 chart success. But it was Fury's backing group The Tornados that stole the show with their mammoth Joe Meek instrumental *Telstar* still sitting at No.1 on that day. Billy Fury's *Because Of Love* had just entered the charts and other acts charting that day were Mike Sarne (*Will I What*), Mark Wynter (*Venus In Blue Jeans*) and Jimmy Justice ('*Aint That Funny*). The bill also included Marty Wilde, Joe Brown and The Bruvvers, The Karl Denver Trio and Peter Jay & The Jaywalkers.

No.1 ON THIS DAY
TELSTAR
The Tornados

GAUMONT : Derby
THE MAMMOTH
STAR SHOW OF 1962
1st Performance at 6-25 p.m.
FRIDAY
OCTOBER **26**
FRONT STALLS 9/6
E 9
No ticket exchanged nor money refunded
THIS PORTION TO BE RETAINED

PROMOTER: Larry Parnes
'The Mammoth Star Show of 1962'

BILLY FURY AND HIS TORNADOS

MARTY WILDE

KARL DENVER TRIO

JOE BROWN & THE BRUVVERS

MIKE SARNE

MARK WYNTER

JIMMY JUSTICE

PETER JAY & THE JAYWALKERS

AL PAIGE (COMPÈRE)

I was there!

26th October 1962
Pauline Sims
Swarkestone, Derby

I didn't get to see this concert but at the time I was working in the cosmetic department of Boots on the corner of St Peters Street and East Street. When a pop package tour came to Derby the stars would sometimes visit the café on the top floor of the store. If they did it would spread around the store like wildfire but we weren't ever allowed to leave our departments and as pop stars didn't often wear make-up in those days there was little chance of seeing them. However, on this particular day I do remember that Marty Wilde walked passed my counter.

LARRY PARNES presents
The **Mammoth STAR SHOW of 1962**
souvenir programme
two shillings

26th October 1962
John Burley
Derby

I was there!

On the day of this concert I literally bumped into the star of the show. In my lunchtime I had spent too long listening to 45s in one of the private listening booths at Dalton's record shop on The Spot and was late for work. I dashed out of the door and bumped straight into a man who was walking past knocking him off his Cuban heel boots and right into the road. All I could say to him as he picked himself up was "You're Billy Fury, I'm so sorry."

The Tornados

26th October 1962

Derby Evening Telegraph

While Billy Fury took the audience by storm during a one-night pop singing stage show at the Gaumont, Derby, it was his own group – the Tornados who raised the roof with their playing of the universally popular Telstar number. Mike Sarne, too, pleased his many admirers in the audience with his still currently popular Come Outside and Will I What?

39

2nd December 1962

Cliff Richard & The Shadows

CLIFF RICHARD & THE SHADOWS

JACKIE TRENT

THE BREAKAWAYS

ALAN RANDALL

THE TREBLETONES

ALAN FIELD (COMPÈRE)

A sixth appearance for Cliff Richard & The Shadows at The Gaumont, Derby. Cliff's double-sided hit *The Next Time/Bachelor Boy* entered the charts later that week and The Shadows *Dance On* a couple of weeks after that. In support was new female vocal trio The Breakaways who went on to become Britain's premier session backing group. The girls previously recorded as Liverpool trio The Vernon Girls who had a hit with *Lover Please* earlier that year. Also in support was Jackie Trent who wouldn't find chart success until 1965 but did so in style with her No.1 *Where Are You Now (My Love)*. Completing the bill were two acts making return visits to the Gaumont - George Formby impersonator Alan Randall and Butlins Holiday Camp favorites The Trebletones. Just a month after this show, Cliff's blockbusting film Summer Holiday had its World Premiere at the Warner Theatre in London's West End.

No.1 ON THIS DAY
FRANK IFIELD
Lovesick Blues

I was there!

2nd December 1962
Lynne Tomlinson (now Lynne Dixon)
The Derbyshire Advertiser

Top British pop star Cliff Richard, accompanied by his own instrumental group, The Shadows, sang to an audience of highly demonstrative fans, at the Gaumont Theatre, on Sunday night. No Cliff Richard show is ever complete without the screams, shouts and wails of appreciation, and Sunday night's appearance was no exception to the rule. As usual, there was not one spare seat to be seen but rather an unusual feature about this audience was that a very large number of mums and dads were there with their teenage daughters and sons. Cliff is now maturing into a very confident and accomplished performer, and this was emphasised by the fact that he no longer wears a shocking pink jacket, but a very smartly tailored dark suit. At regular intervals during his performance, numbers of starry-eyed girls scrambled out of their seats and rushed up towards the stage where they threw their autograph books, and even bouquets, at Cliff's feet. Cliff is very fortunate, of course, in having the talents of the most accomplished instrumental group in Britain behind him, and The Shadows worked doubly hard on Sunday because they did something like a thirty-minute act on their own, as well as accompanying Cliff. Before he was due to go on stage for the first performance, I talked to Cliff, who showed a surprising lack of nerves for a fairly young performer. He spoke of his latest film Summer Holiday, which will receive its London premiere on January 10th.

Cliff Richard in his dressing room with Derbyshire Advertiser reporter Lynne Tomlinson (now Dixon)

41

I was there!

**22nd February 1963
Lynne Tomlinson
(now Lynne Dixon)
The Derbyshire Advertiser**

Besides Joe Brown the show was crammed full of other top-liners such as Jess Conrad, Eden Kane, Susan Maughan and Shane Fenton – names which have rarely appeared together on one bill. Mansfield-born Shane Fenton, backed by the Fentones, proved a great hit with the girls in the audience but to me, his act seemed too much of a carbon copy of many others. Closing the first half of the show were The Tornados who certainly lived up to their title as they played the internationally-popular Telstar and their latest disc Globetrotter. Handsome Jess Conrad immediately won his audience over, but the screams and shouts of appreciation were so deafening, that at times it was difficult to hear what song he was singing. Wearing a sparkling gold dress, dark-eyed Susan Maughan brought a touch of glamour into the show and Eden Kane seemed to have improved in his singing since I last saw him in Derby. But it was Joe Brown and the Bruvvers that the audience were clearly waiting for, and they rose to highest expectations, proving the highlight of the show. Bouncing with fun and energy blonde-haired Cockney Joe hopped, skipped, jumped through his act in a way that could not be ignored.

Chapter 5

1963 First signs that British Pop was about to take over the World

22nd February 1963

Joe Brown

The first Gaumont package tour of 1963 kicked-off with another bumper bill. Despite thirteen different acts taking to the stage, promotor Larry Parnes called his show 'Your Lucky Stars'. Joe Brown headlined although many of the artists could have claimed equal billing. The Tornados *Globetrotter*, the follow-up to their worldwide smash *Telstar*, was in the Top 20 and four months earlier Susan Maughan had reached No.3 with her cover of *Bobby's Girl*. Top-of-the-bill Joe Brown had back-to-back Top 10 hits with *It Only Took A Minute* and *That's What Love Will Do* which were both still in the charts on that day. Making return visits to Derby were Eden Kane, who had a Top 10 with *I Don't Know Why* the previous year, and Shane Fenton, later to become Alvin Stardust, with his backing group The Fentones who had enjoyed minor instrumental hits of their own. Also on the bill were Jess Conrad, another return visit to the Gaumont for Peter Jay & The Jaywalkers and bringing novelty to the show was TV favourite Rolf Harris, famous for his international 1960 hit *Tie Me Kangaroo Down, Sport*.

No.1 ON THIS DAY
JET HARRIS AND TONY MEEHAN
Diamonds

PROMOTER: Larry Parnes 'Your Lucky Stars'
JOE BROWN
SUSAN MAUGHAN
THE TORNADOS
EDEN KANE
SHANE FENTON & THE FENTONES
JESS CONRAD
ROLF HARRIS
PETER JAY & THE JAYWALKERS
DARYL QUIST
PETER LODGE
MIKE & TONY NEVITT
THE DIGGEROOS
AL PAIGE (COMPÈRE)

GAUMONT
DERBY
2nd PERF. 8-40
FRIDAY
FEBRUARY 22
Front Stalls
9/6
B36
TO BE GIVEN UP

GAUMONT : Derby
YOUR LUCKY STARS
2nd Performance at 8-40 p.m.
FRIDAY
FEBRUARY 22
FRONT STALLS 9/6
B36
No ticket exchanged nor money refunded
THIS PORTION TO BE RETAINED

17th March 1963

Helen Shapiro

Since making her Derby debut in April of the previous year, Helen Shapiro added just one more Top 10 hit to her short, but spectacular period as a major British artist. Her *Little Miss Lonely* which made No.8 in August 1962 was to be her final Top 20 placing. Second on the bill were ex-Shadows duo Jet Harris & Tony Meehan who had made the top spot in January with *Diamonds* which was still in the charts on the day of the concert. They too went on to enjoy a short but highly successful time at the top with two further Top 10 hits later that year. Also in support was Danny Williams, famous for his 1961 chart topping cover of the classic *Moon River*, and Bristol group The Kestrels which provided vocal backing for several early 60s British recording stars and whose members had included songwriting team Roger Cook and Roger Greenaway. The compère was Dave Allen, his last Derby appearance before leaving Britain to find fame in Australia, after which he returned to become a major British TV star.

No.1 ON THIS DAY
CLIFF RICHARD AND THE SHADOWS
Summer Holiday

GRANADA   March 1963

I was there!

17th March 1963
Lynne Tomlinson
(now Lynne Dixon)
The Derbyshire Advertiser

With the voice of a mature blues singer, and the technique of an artiste with twice her experience, little Miss Helen Shapiro gave an outstanding performance when she appeared at the Gaumont, Derby, on Sunday night. A slightly-built figure in a full-skirted yellow dress, which contrasted well with her dark hair, Helen was at her best in every way. With a powerful voice that was always note-perfect, Helen sounded terrific, whether singing pop songs or standards. One of this country's up-and-coming young singers, Danny Williams, gave a tremendous performance, and was on stage for nearly 30 minutes. Jet Harris and Tony Meehan have been to Derby several times before, as members of The Shadows, but on Sunday they appeared as a team for the first time. Between shows, Helen relaxed in her dressing room, strummed her banjo, and spoke of her recent world tours. She has recently come back from America, where she visited Nashville, and made a number of records. She did not meet Elvis there, but did the next best thing – she sang with his backing group, The Jordanaires.

23rd April 1963

Billy Fury

This show was entitled 'An Evening With Billy Fury' and it was the British singer's third top-of-the-bill appearance in Derby. However, his backing group The Tornados had enjoyed more success that year with their Top 10 hit *Globe-Trotter*, the follow up to their international chart topper *Telstar*. Fury shared his evening with support acts Mike Preston and Dickie Pride. Preston made his name in 1959 with his cover of *Mr Blue* but his 1961 Top 20 hit *Marry Me* saw the end to his chart successes. Happily he went on to establish a long and more successful career as a film and TV actor. Although a regular performer on Jack Good's TV Rock'n'Roll shows, Dickie Pride had only managed to make the charts once with *Primrose Lane* in 1959.

No.1 ON THIS DAY
GERRY AND THE PACEMAKERS
How Do You Do It

PROMOTER: Larry Parnes
'An Evening With Billy Fury'

BILLY FURY

THE TORNADOS

MIKE PRESTON

DICKIE PRIDE

MIKE & TONY NEVITT

THE ECHOES

LARRY BURNS (COMPĒRE)

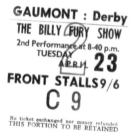

GAUMONT : Derby
THE BILLY FURY SHOW
2nd Performance at 8-40 p.m.
TUESDAY
APRIL **23**
FRONT STALLS 9/6
C 9
No ticket exchanged nor money refunded
THIS PORTION TO BE RETAINED

Larry Parnes presents
AN EVENING WITH BILLY FURY
SOUVENIR PROGRAMME

I was there!

23rd April 1963
Joe Gunther
Willington, Derby

At the tender age of 15 this was my first Gaumont pop concert, but there was nothing tender about my behaviour back then. As soon as I left school and got a job I left home and shared a flat in town with my older friend, Barry Clee, who was a notorious Teddy Boy. Barry was a Liverpudlian and decided that he wanted to see the performance of his fellow Scouser, Billy Fury, at the Gaumont. We sat high up in the balcony and, as 'Teds', it was our job to be as threatening and irreverent as possible. So after one of Fury's tender ballads Barry stood up from his seat and shouted "Get back to the Dingle!" which is a district of Liverpool.

14th May 1963

The Four Seasons and John Leyton

Promoted as 'All Stars 63' this show was something of a 'swan song' for the artists on the bill with 1963 being the year when most of them stalled as far as chart success went.

No.1 ON THIS DAY

GERRY AND THE PACEMAKERS
How Do You Do It

John Leyton was originally headlining the tour but before it reached Derby The Four Seasons were added to the line-up and usurped him as the bill toppers having had back-to-back hits with *Sherry*, *Big Girls Don't Cry* and *Walk Like A Man*. John Leyton was still managing to draw a reasonable crowd on the back of his 1961 hits as were his main support acts Mike Berry, Billie Davis, Jet Harris & Tony Meehan and Duffy Power. However, other than the Four Seasons, this tour turned out to be a showcase of the early 60s British hit makers that were being hounded out of the charts by the 'Mersey Beat' boom. Also on the bill was Daily Mail journalist-come-singer Bick Ford along with Don Spencer and the XL5 who had a minor hit a month earlier with *Fireball*, the theme from the science fiction children's cartoon TV show.

PROMOTER: Robert Stigwood
'All Stars 63'

**THE FOUR SEASONS
JOHN LEYTON**

MIKE BERRY &
THE INNOCENTS

BILLIE DAVIS

JET HARRIS &
TONY MEEHAN

DUFFY POWER

BILLY DOYLE

DON SPENCER

BICK FORD

THE X-L FIVE

THE HI-FI'S

GRAZINA

GAUMONT
DERBY

2nd PERF. 8-40

TUESDAY
MAY 14

Front Stalls
8/6

B35

TO BE GIVEN UP

GAUMONT : Derby

ALL STARS '63

2nd Performance at 8-40 p.m.
TUESDAY
MAY 14

FRONT STALLS 8/6

B35

No ticket exchanged nor money refunded
THIS PORTION TO BE RETAINED

*Frankie Valli and
The Four Season
serenade Derbyshire
Advertiser reporter
Lynne Tomlinson
(now Dixon)*

I was there!

14th May 1963
Lynne Tomlinson
(now Lynne Dixon)
The Derbyshire Advertiser

Add an excitingly different sound to a polished performance and a considerable amount of real talent, and you have the Four Seasons – the tremendously popular vocal group who are at present making a brief tour of England. And what a fine reception the Seasons got at the Gaumont, Derby, on Tuesday, when they topped the bill of All Stars '63 with John Leyton. The audience clearly recognised a truly talented group when they saw one, and showed their appreciation by not screaming all the way through the Seasons' act. Certainly one of the most swinging groups on the pop scene at the moment, these four Italian-looking boys from New Jersey went through all their smash hits and each time came up to my highest expectations. Opening their act with their first big hit Sherry, the Seasons went on to sing their other big records – Big Girls Don't Cry and Walk Like a Man. And they sounded every bit as good as they do on record. The fantastically high-pitched voice which dominates all their records and always picks out the melody, belongs to 23-years-old Frankie Valli, a softly spoken, slightly-built young man. The background chorus is provided by Nick Massi, Tommy De Vito and tall, handsome Bob Gaudio. During the interval they told me how pleased they had been with their reception in Derby. Sharing top billing with the Seasons was John Leyton, and this fair-haired figure dressed in a silvery grey suit and white shoes, had the fans shouting for more. He sang a medley of big hits which included Hallelujah I Love Her So and What'd I Say, then went through all his own hits, Johnny Remember Me, Wild Wind, Son This is She and his latest disc, Cupboard Love. Also on the bill were Jet Harris and Tony Meehan, with an act that was almost identical to their last appearance in Derby a few weeks ago. Mike Berry, who proved very popular and has probably got a bright future ahead of him; Billie Davis, who shouted her way through her act; Daily Mail reporter Bick Ford; Duffy Power; Don Spencer and the XL5; and Grazina.

Everly Brothers

PROMOTER: Don Arden
EVERLY BROTHERS
LITTLE RICHARD
BO DIDDLEY
ROLLING STONES
JULIE GRANT
MICKIE MOST
THE FLINTSTONES
BOB BAIN (COMPÈRE)

This was perhaps the most memorable and talked about of all the Gaumont pop concerts. Topping the bill of this nationwide tour were the Everly Brothers and Bo Diddley. But by the time it reached Derby, Little Richard had been added to the bill and The Rolling Stones were the hottest new band in the land with their first hit, a cover of Chuck Berry's *Come On*, still in the charts on that day. Some of the audience were still chanting the group's name after they had closed the first half and even while the top-of-the-bill artists were performing - a sure sign of things to come for the Stones. But that's not to say that the established stars didn't please. It was a return visit for The Everly Brothers having appeared at the Gaumont, Derby in April 1960 and although their popularity was being challenged by the 'British Invasion' the brothers still headlined. Rock'n'Roll legend Little Richard put in a storming performance playing part of his set with his foot on top of his grand piano and, at one stage, stripping to the waist and climbing on top of it. Bo Diddley was one of the black Amercian R&B stars who influenced the new generation of British groups including the Beatles and the Stones. Thanks to this tour, on the day he performed in Derby, his first UK hit *Pretty Thing* had just entered the charts. Bo Diddley often included women in his band and on this occasion his act featured the glamourous Norma-Jean Wofford, known as The Duchess. Also on the bill was Mickie Most who went on to become one of the most successful record producers in Britain. At this time he was a relatively unknown solo singer who charted for just one week earlier that year with *Mr. Porter*, his only taste of chart success as a performer. Completing the line-up of this historic Derby Gaumont show were The Flinstones and British singer Julie Grant who had two minor hits earlier that year with a cover of *Up On The Roof* and *Count On Me*.

THE ROLLING STONES DECCA
YOU BETTER MOVE ON
POISON IVY
BYE BYE JOHNNY
MONEY

No.1 ON THIS DAY
BRIAN POOLE AND THE TREMELOES
Do You Love Me

I was there!

11th October 1963
Barbara Zoppi (nee Cater)
Chaddesden, Derby

I call myself the original 'Rock Chick' because my first concert was in 1963 at the tender age of 14 and now, in my mid-sixties, I still travel the country to see live bands. That first concert at the Gaumont, Derby was headlined by The Everly Brothers and Little Richard but it was more memorable for me because the Rolling Stones closed the first half of the show. Despite their casual appearance I remember them all bowing after their performance which I thought was a little strange. But for me the special guest Bo Diddley and The Duchess were the stars of the show. I went with my older friend, Susan Cook, and we sat in the middle of the stalls. Susan was so embarrassed when Little Richard took his shirt off during his performance. She said "Ooo! if my mum knew he was going to do that she wouldn't have let me come". My dad picked us up after the show but we didn't mention the strip show.

Bo Diddley and Little Richard stage an impromptu rehearsal in the Gaumont dressing room
Photo: Derby Telegraph

I was there!

11th October 1963
Lynne Tomlinson
(now Lynne Dixon)
The Derbyshire Advertiser

Anyone who has seen Little Richard chanting on top of his piano, or dancing wildly before hundreds of yelling youngsters, as he strips off his jacket, tie and shoes, might be surprised to learn that this man's ambition is to become an evangelist – like Billy Graham! But this is what Little Richard told me as he cooled off quietly in his dressing room at the Gaumont, Derby, on Friday night, after giving one of the most fantastic performances I have ever seen at a stage show. No one was surprised when he leaped on to the top of his piano, but it came as quite a shock when he jumped off the stage, threw off his tie, jacket and shoes, and began dancing with a girl who sat nearby. In contrast, the Everly Brothers gave a far less flamboyant performance, but nevertheless came up to highest expectations. The much-talked-about Bo Diddley was a slight disappointment because it was so difficult to tell what he was singing about. Also featured in this noisy, colourful, earthy act were Bo's half-sister, The Duchess, who looked glamorous in skin-tight silver lame pants, and Jerome Green, a gifted maracas player. A touch of the Liverpool sound was brought to the show by The Rolling Stones, who seemed to verge on the ridiculous at times. Their hairstyles were just a bit too exaggerated, I thought, but they were fun and went down well with the audience, Come On was the only number that I found possible to distinguish in the general din.

11th October 1963
John Burley
Chaddesden, Derby

I once got into trouble when I was home on leave from my Army unit in West Germany in 1963. Posters suddenly appeared on billboards advertising a forthcoming live Rock'n'Roll show featuring USA favorites at the Gaumont. Top of the bill were the Everly Brothers along with Little Richard and Bo Diddley. The show also introduced an up and coming British band, The Rolling Stones. The date was two or three weeks after my leave was due to end. But my mind was made up - how could I miss a show like that? So, off I went to my doctor and obtained a sick note. My younger sister and I got tickets for that unforgettable show. But by that time my sick note had expired and I was listed as AWOL (absent without leave). I was duly picked up and taken into custody, spending two days in St Mary's Gate police cells before an Army escort took me to Borden in Hampshire for two more days in custody. I was then escorted to Buller Barracks, Aldershot, and locked up there for almost a week, after which I was taken back to my unit at Bielefeld, West Germany. I spent a further 28 days in detention, plus loss of pay, all for the sake of my love for Rock'n'Roll and its heroes. But I have never regretted it.

11th October 1963
Alan Kinsey
Vouleme, Poitou-Charentes, France

It's 1963 and I'm fourteen-years-old. My older sister Pat is bonkers about the Everly Brothers. I like them too, even though a lot of their stuff seems a bit girly. One evening Pat asks me if I'd like to go and see the Everly Brothers with her and my other sister Sheila. I decline, thinking that they're probably a bit old fashioned for me, but a few days later I'm at the bus stop with my school mates and I'm reading the Melody Maker. Suddenly I spot an ad for the Everly's tour and see that the Rolling Stones are opening for them. I'd recently bought the Stones first single, a cover of Chuck Berry's Come On, and was already a big fan. That evening I tell my sisters that I've changed my mind and I'd love to go with them. Then later, and to my delight and amazement, I read that the promoters have decided to fly in Little Richard and Bo Diddley from the USA. Memories of the actual concert at the Gaumont cinema in Derby are vague now. The 'Stones had obviously progressed from the sharp suits that their manager Andrew Oldham had insisted they wear. Leather trousers and suede jerkins seemed to be in evidence. I recall dozens of Teddy Boys and Greasers standing in front of the stage going mental while Little Richard performed. Half way though his last number he took off his shirt and threw it into the audience to the shrieks of the already hysterical girls. I was shocked and amazed to see he was wearing a vest exactly like the one my dad wore while he shaved himself at the kitchen sink at home. The same Teds and Greasers booed and whistled throughout the poor Everly Brothers set at the end of the show. Their time was over.

I was there!

11th October 1963
Pat Haldenby
Littleover, Derby

On the day of this concert I was only 13 and too young to go to the show. So, together with a couple of friends of mine, Jane and Helen, we caught the bus into town after school and camped outside the Gaumont stage door in the hope of seeing some of the stars. My parents gave me permission as long as I was back by 6pm. We caught the bus into town from Homelands school in Village Street armed with our autograph books, pens and sandwiches. The stage door was at the back of the cinema on Osmaston Road and after a while we heard the doors being unlocked and to our excitement Mick Jagger popped out with some of the other Stones. He seemed to be very much in charge and asked us where they could get something to eat. We managed to overcome our initial excitement and led them towards the Spot and pointed towards the centre of town. I managed to find my voice and asked Mick Jagger for his autograph. Before we were joined by other star-struck autograph hunters Mick turned to me and asked if he could borrow my Biro. After getting their signatures they disappeared down St Peters Street and we rushed back to the stage door encouraged by our initial success. Eventually a doorman came out and asked if we would like him to take our books inside to get more autographs from the rest of the cast who were busy doing sound checks. After a while he returned with my book complete with the signatures of the Everly Brothers who were top of the bill. We caught the bus back home happy with the additions to our precious autograph books.

Bo Diddley with 'The Duchess' and Jerome
Photo: Derby Telegraph

22nd November 1963

Billy Fury

This event was titled 'The Big Star Show' but is best remembered by the Derby audience as the day when US President John F Kennedy was assassinated with the news breaking a few hours before the curtain went up for the 2nd performance. At the time, when pop music was rapidly changing in favour of the Mersey influenced groups, the line-up looked rather dated. Despite this obvious

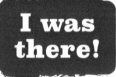
No.1 ON THIS DAY
GERRY AND THE PACEMAKERS
You'll Never Walk Alone

PROMOTER: Larry Parnes 'The Big Star Show'
BILLY FURY
JOE BROWN
KARL DENVER TRIO
THE TORNADOS
MARTY WILDE
DARYL QUIST
DICKIE PRIDE
THE RAMBLERS
LARRY BURNS (COMPÈRE)

'sea change' in musical tastes Larry Parnes continued to send his stable of artists out on the road. Although Billy Fury headlined the show it featured four other artists who could have claimed equal billing - Joe Brown, The Karl Denver Trio, The Tornados and Marty Wilde - but significantly none were charting at that time. Fury had presented his own Derby show earlier that year with some of these artists and this was his 4th appearance at the Gaumont. Since his previous visit he had enjoyed a Top 10 that summer with his appropriately titled hit *In Summer*. The other 'Big Stars' completing the bill were Dickie Pride, Canadian singer/actor Daryl Quist and The Ramblers.

I was there!

22nd November 1963
Cherrylin Stockley (nee Smith)
Hinckley, Leicestershire

My best friend Beti persuaded me to go to this show because she really liked Billy Fury and as far as the Gaumont pop concerts were concerned we were almost attached at the hip and went on to see over fifteen shows together. But my memories of that evening were totally clouded by the world shattering news just before we set off that President J F Kennedy had been shot. I asked my dad if he thought the show would still go on and whether or not we should go. He was a very practical man and said "Well you might as well go because you can't change what's already happened". I have always remembered his words and often reflect on how true that is in life. As we settled into our seats on row E, quite near the front, the compère came on stage and asked the audience to show a degree of respect in view of the sad news. The proceedings were quite subdued before it all started but as they say 'the show must go on!' and the performers managed to raise the spirits. Beti's only clear memory of the show is that Billy Fury sat on the front of the stage and sang a ballad.

GAUMONT : Derby
BILLY FURY SHOW
2nd Performance at 8-40 p.m.
FRIDAY
NOVEMBER **22**
FRONT STALLS 10/6
E18
No ticket exchanged nor money refunded
THIS PORTION TO BE RETAINED

Chapter 6

1964 British beat groups claim their territory

24th February 1964

Joe Brown & His Bruvvers

PROMOTER: Larry Parnes 'Your Lucky Stars'

JOE BROWN & HIS BRUVVERS

THE CRYSTALS

JOHNNY KIDD AND THE PIRATES

HEINZ AND THE SAINTS

DARYL QUIST

MIKE PRESTON

MANFRED MANN

KEVIN KIRK

AL PAIGE (COMPÈRE)

Another Larry Parnes 'Your Lucky Stars' show and, according to records, the last of his promotions to visit the Gaumont. Significantly his line-up included Manfred Mann, one of the many emerging R&B influenced British groups which had taken over the charts by then. Although pop package stalwart Joe Brown topped the bill the Derby audience were treated to their first sight of one of the Phil Spectre-produced American girl groups. The Crystals from New York had enjoyed three Top 20 hits the previous year with *He's A Rebel*, *Da Doo Ron Ron* and *Then He Kissed Me*. Manfred Mann whose Top 10 hit *5-4-3-2-1*, the theme song to TV's 'Ready Steady Go', was in the charts at No.5. Making his first visit to the Gaumont was old Rock'n'Roller, Johnny Kidd with his Pirates who had charted the previous year with a more modern sounding *I'll Never Get Over You*. Also on the bill was Joe Meek protégé Heinz, the former bass player with The Tornados. German-born Heinz had reached No.5 the previous year with *Just Like Eddie*, a tribute to Eddie Cochran who died in a car crash in April 1960 while making the journey between Bristol and London on a similar tour. Making return visits were Canadian, Daryl Quist who had been part of the last Gaumont package tour just three months earlier, and Mike Preston.

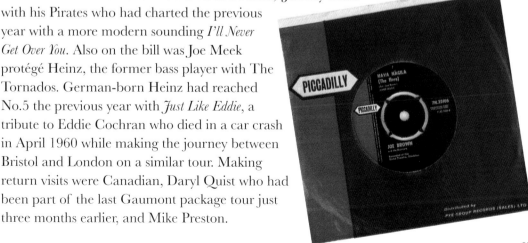

I was there!

24th February 1964
Pat Haldenby
Littleover, Derby

At 14 years old I was still too young to attend the show but, as on previous occasions, my friends and I managed to get down to the stage door of the Gaumont after school. I was hoping to see Manfred Mann who were in the hit parade with 5-4-3-2-1, the signature tune to TVs Ready Steady Go. We waited patiently outside the doors until one girl in the small crowd had the idea of knocking on one of the dressing room windows. She knocked hard and shouted "Is anyone in there?" A voice answered "Yes" so the girl asked "Who are you? Are you famous?" The voice shouted back with an American accent "We're The Crystals". So we all pushed our autograph books through the open window which they kindly signed. A little while later, to my delight, Paul Jones and some other members of Manfred Mann came out and signed our books too.

24th February 1964
Shaun (Skeg) Walton
Vancouver, Canada

After I moved from Skegness to 'digs' in Sinfin, Derby to start an apprenticeship at Rolls-Royce I was able to attend quite a few Gaumont pop concerts. This show particularly sticks out in my mind and especially the image of Joe Brown performing his show-piece where he played the instrumental Hava Nagila

HEINZ

with his guitar behind his head. For some reason I was particularly impressed with the red lining to his suit jacket which flapped open as he picked out the melody. As for Manfred Mann, I just remember Paul Jones getting a bit annoyed with some of the audience. He was trying to bring the tempo down and perform a semi-acoustic version of Bob Dylan's With God On Our Side but the noise from the auditorium was making it virtually impossible. He suddenly halted proceedings and announced "Will you please tell those 'rivers' out there to shut-up! You know who the 'rivers' are – small in the head and big in the mouth." A strange metaphor I thought.

Larry Parnes presents

Your Lucky Stars

Souvenir Programme   **Two Shillings**

15th March 1964

Billy J Kramer

For this show Beatles manager Brian Epstein was joint promoter with Arthur Howes; a sure sign that the 'Mersey Beat' groups were taking over the package tours as well as the charts.

All the acts hailed from Liverpool with the exception of US star Gene Pitney whose Top 10 *That Girl Belongs To Yesterday* entered the charts that week. Cilla Black made her Derby debut on a very special day for her with *Anyone Who Had A Heart* rising to No.1 in the charts. Despite this, Billy J Kramer topped the bill and his fourth hit *Little Children* knocked Cilla off the top spot at the end of that week. Also in support were The Swinging Blue Jeans whose No.2 *Hippy Hippy Shake* had just left the charts only to be replaced at the end of the week with their second hit Good Golly Miss Molly. Completing the line-up were two of Liverpool's favourite groups - The Remo Four and The Escorts.

No.1 ON THIS DAY
CILLA BLACK
Anyone Who Had A Heart

PROMOTERS: Arthur Howes and Brian Epstein

BILLY J KRAMER
GENE PITNEY
SWINGING BLUE JEANS
CILLA BLACK
REMO FOUR
THE ESCORTS
BILLY BURDEN (COMPÈRE)

I was there!

**15th March 1964
Pauline Sims
(nee Byard)
Swarkestone, Derby**

Although this concert mainly featured the Liverpool groups I persuaded my boyfriend, Brian (now my husband) to take me to see my heart-throb Gene Pitney. The thing I remember most about the show was how shocked I was to see Cilla Black's bright red hair. I had only ever seen her on television which of course was in black and white in those days. I still have the programme which also only showed black and white photographs.

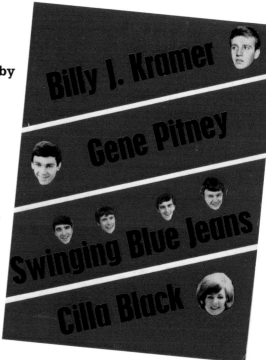

Billy J. Kramer
Gene Pitney
Swinging Blue Jeans
Cilla Black

I was there!

15th March 1964
Patrick Flood
Alvaston, Derby

As an 18 year old apprentice welder at Aiton's in Sinfin Lane I was always short of cash. At that time my sister Mary was an usherette at the Gaumont cinema and she managed to get me a part-time job as a Junior Doorman to supplement my meagre wages. I ended up earning more in three nights there than I did for a whole week at my day-job. My main duties were to patrol the back-stage areas of the theatre and especially the stage doors which opened out onto Osmaston Road. This was to make sure that no one was sneaking in without paying. This job was particular difficult during the pop concerts as throngs of girls would congregate outsides the doors in an effort to see their heart-throbs arrive and leave. On the night of the Billy J Kramer concert three policemen from Full Street were detailed to help control the crowds and three knocks from the bobbies was my cue to open up. As I did there was a massive surge from what must have been hundreds of girls and I was met by a dishevelled Gene Pitney and the bobbies with their helmets askew. The girls were shouting "Gene, Gene" and fighting to get their hands on any part of his anatomy. I was the only one that did as I dragged Mr Pitney inside and he turned to me and said "Hey Bud! Do you get danger money for this?" My sister, who was a huge Pitney fan, had asked me to get his autograph and after the show he presented me with a large photograph, duly signed 'To Pat'. I had to hide it behind a radiator and finish my duties but when I returned it had disappeared. So I was, sadly, unable to repay her for getting me this exciting job with all its wonderful memories.

I was there!

15th March 1964
Neil Hallam
Belper, Derbyshire

I was working for Raymonds News Agency in Derby and had just taken over as the Melody Maker's local correspondent when Gene Pitney came to town. The paper's northern news editor sent me along to confront the American with a rumour he claimed was "sweeping the music business" - that Pitney had secretly married Dusty Springfield. I was warned "You might get your head bitten off. He's a bit full of himself" but apart from a somewhat patronising attitude and some heavy sarcasm there was no real problem. He issued a flat denial, of course, and later revelations about Dusty made the rumour seem even more bizarre. As I was leaving, Pitney asked me where I had bought the trenchcoat I was wearing and I thought this was more sarcasm. He denied that this was the case, insisted that he had been looking for something similar for ages and got one of his acolytes to get pen and paper and take down the name of Cunningham's gents' outfitters. I'm still not sure whether he was being sarky but the next time I was in Cunningham's I asked if Gene Pitney had been in and they looked at me gone out.

22nd April 1964

Adam Faith

Still managing to top the bill, Adam Faith was one of the 'old school' early 60s stars that had attempted to emulate the 'Mersey Beat' sound with the help of his backing group The Roulettes. He made the Top 10 at the back end of 1963 with his fresher sounding Chris Andrews song *The First Time* but only managed minor success thereafter and this would be the fourth and last time the Gaumont's velvet curtains came down on Adam Faith. Another early 60s favourite Eden Kane was making his second Gaumont appearance and was also clinging on to success during the beat group invasion. However, he had managed a Top 10 hit with *Boy's Cry* the previous month. The Searchers were continuing to storm the charts and their third No.1 in less than 12 months *Don't Throw Your Love Away* had entered the charts that week. Also on the bill was another emerging act - Dave Berry & The Cruisers -who would notch-up their biggest hit *The Crying Game* a few months later. In support were The Undertakers who had a minor hit that month with *Just A Little Bit*, and British girl singer Lorriene Gray.

No.1 ON THIS DAY
THE BEATLES Can't Buy Me Love

PROMOTERS: Tito Burns & Peter Walsh

ADAM FAITH

THE SEARCHERS

EDEN KANE

DAVE BERRY & THE CRUISERS

THE ROULETTES

THE UNDERTAKERS

LORRIENE GRAY

DAVE CURTISS & THE TREMORS

BARRY O'DOWDE

Dave Berry

GAUMONT DERBY
2nd Perf. 8-40
WEDNESDAY
APRIL 22
Front Stalls 10/6
E37
TO BE GIVEN UP

GAUMONT : Derby
THE ADAM FAITH SHOW
2nd Performance 8-40 p.m.
WEDNESDAY APRIL 22
FRONT STALLS 10/6
E37
No ticket exchanged nor money refunded
THIS PORTION TO BE RETAINED

Singer Lorriene Gray with
Eden Kane and Adam Faith.
Photo: Eric Chapman

I was there!

22nd April 1964
Eric Chapman
Stapleford, Nottingham

At the time of the Gaumont's pop package tours I was working as a compositor at the local weekly paper - The Derbyshire Advertiser. In my spare time I was a keen amateur photographer with several cameras and a well-equipped dark room at home. The professional photographer on the newspaper didn't like pop music or working in the evenings so the editor asked if I'd like to cover some of the concerts. I loved all types of music and jumped at the chance to go along to photograph the stars. I arrived early for the Adam Faith show and started knocking on dressing room doors at random – none had names or even a star. The first door I knocked on was answered by Adam Faith who let me in after I explained why I was there. He was all alone and seemed glad to have someone to talk to. I only took one shot because the newspaper wouldn't pay for my film. Then we started talking about body building which was another interest of mine. We just chatted about weight training and other methods of physical exercise and not about the 'music business' as I expected. I think he was suffering from pre-concert nerves being all alone in a dressing room and he seemed so eager to talk to a complete stranger about something other than his imminent performance. After that Eden Kane took pity on me because of my minimal amount of film so he very kindly organised a group shot with Adam Faith, Liverpool group The Undertakers and a really nice girl singer I'd not heard of called Lorriene Grey.

Photo: Eric Chapman

Dave Clark Five

PROMOTER: Arthur Howes
DAVE CLARK FIVE
THE HOLLIES
MARK WYNTER
THE KINKS
THE MOJOS
THE TREBLETONES
FRANK BERRY (COMPÈRE)

The line-up for this tour was confirmation that the British beat groups had taken over the pop scene and that is wasn't just the Liverpool bands that were finding success. North London group The Dave Clark Five topped the bill. In January that year they knocked The Beatles

No.1 ON THIS DAY
THE SEARCHERS
Don't Throw Your Love Away

I Want To Hold Your Hand off the top of the charts with their single *Glad All Over* and their follow-up *Bits And Pieces* had made No.2. Manchester group The Hollies whose Top 10 hit *Just One Look* was still in the charts were second on the bill. Up-and-coming London group The Kinks were also in support, just three months prior to equaling the success of the headliners with their No.1 smash *You Really Got Me*. This show wouldn't have been complete without a Liverpool group and The Mojos did the honours on the back of their only Top.10 hit *Everything's Alright* which was at No.9 on that day. Completing the bill, but sounding rather out of place, were early 60s tour favorite Mark Wynter along with The Trebletones who were returning to Derby after being in support at two Derby Gaumont shows in 1962.

9th May 1964
Lynne Tomlinson
(now Lynne Dixon)
The Derbyshire Advertiser

If you can imagine about 4,000 arms waving and the same number of feet stamping, giving an overall impression of a theatre shaking, then you may have some small idea of the incredible impact made by the Dave Clark Five in Derby on Saturday. There had been the usual amount of screaming at the Gaumont, when The Mojos, The Kinks and The Hollies were on stage. The young audience became more and more frenzied, however, as Mark Wynter's act drew to a close, and the yells of "We want Dave" were ear-splitting. The screams reached fever-pitch when Dave and the boys finally appeared, and the young girls in the audience gave the group quite the most fantastic reception I have seen in Derby. Wearing their now distinctive high-collared white shirts, tailored black jackets, cream trousers and black high-heeled boots, the one striking feature about the Dave Clark Five is their immaculate appearance. It was during those two bouncy numbers, Glad All Over and Bits and Pieces, however that the theatre reverberated with all those thudding feet. Drummer Dave led the stamping on stage and everyone in the audience soon caught on. Backstage, looking more Latin than ever, Dave told me that his follow-up to Bits and Pieces will be See That She's Mine, coupled with Because, to be released on May 22nd. "This will again be an up-tempo number without all the stamping," he said.

9th May 1964
Patrick Flood
Alvaston, Derby

Looking after the safety of the stars was one of my duties when I was a young doorman at the Gaumont pop concerts. I was stationed just inside the stage doors which opened onto Osmaston Road where there would always be a crowd of screaming girls. With the help of the odd police presence on the other side I had to oversee the exit and entry of the artists. The Dave Clark Five were top of the bill on this occasion and, while one of the support acts was performing, a member of the Dave Clark Five (I'm not sure which one but it wasn't

Dave Clark) asked me to open up and direct him to the Neptune pub. I said 'You must be joking, you'll get mobbed and you probably won't get back in time for your performance'. He insisted and said that he had to meet someone there and that it would be ok. He was wearing a big coat over his stage outfit and he proceeded to turn the collar up and assure me that if he wandered out into the crowd instead of making a dash for it, it would be like 'reverse psychology'. So against my better judgement I opened up and off he went. It must have worked because after a few minutes the bobbies knocked three times and he strolled back in and handed me a bottle of beer for my trouble.

Cliff Richard & The Shadows

PROMOTER:
Leslie Grade

CLIFF RICHARD & THE SHADOWS
★★★★★★★★★★★★★★★★★★★★★★
FAYE FISHER
★★★★★★★★★★★★★★★★★★★★★★
JOHNNY HAWKINS & ORCHESTRA
★★★★★★★★★★★★★★★★★★★★★★
FRANK BERRY (COMPÈRE)
★★★★★★★★★★★★★★★★★★★★★★

Despite the British beat group boom Cliff Richard & The Shadows managed to hold their own on the package tour circuit and this was their seventh appearance at the Gaumont Derby. Cliff and the Shads were by far the most popular artists to have ever graced its stage and on this day Cliff's *The Twelfth Of Never* was climbing to an eventual No.8 in the charts. However, The Shadows were having less success against the new-wave R&B groups and would only make No.22 with their latest offering *Rhythm & Greens* despite its witty title. Besides The Shadows, Cliff's backing was augmented by Johnny Hawkins & Orchestra and the only support act was singer Faye Fisher who was billed as 'The New Singing Sensation' and later that year was featured on two tracks of the Cliff and The Shadows LP soundtrack of the pantomime Aladdin and His Wonderful Lamp. The Norrie Paramore produced pantomime ran at the London Palladium from December 1964 but after that nothing much was heard of Miss Fisher despite the positive prediction.

No.1 ON THIS DAY
ROY ORBISON
Oh Pretty Woman

7th November 1964

The Animals

This Don Arden show confirmed that the curtain had finally come down on the old style early 60s pop stars. Billed as R'n'B '64 it was headlined by the Animals whose international hit *House Of The Rising Sun* went straight to No.1 in July that year. In support was American R&B singer Tommy Tucker who had a hit earlier that year with *Hi-Heel Sneakers*. Also on the bill was a relatively unknown Elkie Brooks who wouldn't find the charts until 1977 with *Pearl's A Singer* which started a run of success lasting well into the late 80s. Perhaps the only 'odd man out' on the show was American Rock'n'Roller Carl Perkins whose only UK chart hit was in 1956 with the original of *Blue Suede Shoes*. Also performing and providing backing for the American performers were The Nashville Teens whose Top 10 hit *Google Eye* was in the charts on that day. There was also an interesting compère that night - Canadian comedian Ray Cameron who was the father of TV stand-up star Michael McIntyre and who committed suicide in 1993.

No.1 ON THIS DAY
ROY ORBISON
Oh Pretty Woman

PROMOTER: Don Arden R'n'B '64
THE ANIMALS
CARL PERKINS
TOMMY TUCKER
ELKIE BROOKS
PLEBS
NASHVILLE TEENS
QUOTATIONS
RAY CAMERON (COMPÈRE)

I was there!

7th November 1964
Patrick Flood
Alvaston, Derby

One of my duties as Junior Doorman at the Gaumont cinema was to check that all the fire exits were closed and secure. But it was more about making sure that people couldn't get in rather than ensuring a safe exit for the audience in the case of an emergency. They had togged me out in a commissionaires uniform which was far too big for me. It consisted of a long burgundy coloured coat complete with gold braided epaulettes under which I had to tuck my pristine, white gloves - not a very trendy look for a skinny 18-year-old youth. During this show when I was doing my rounds and while the Animals were on stage I came across around a dozen girls outside their dressing room. I asked them what they were doing and how had they managed to get in, but they just said they were queuing for autographs. I told them they'd have to leave immediately or I'd be in big trouble. But I felt a bit mean throwing them out so before they left I told them to put their names in their books and I'd try to get some signatures. I enlisted the help of some of my colleagues and the girls were able to collect their books from the box-office the next day, complete with new autographs.

I was there!

7th November 1964
Joe Gunther
Willington, Derby

By 1964, when I was about 17, I had changed from my early 60s Teddy Boy-influence image to follow the 'mod' look which was sweeping the country. I was friendly with a local character, Tommy McNamara, who owned a really flashy American car – a white Chevrolet Corvair. We would often cruise around girl-watching and park outside some of the teenage hot-spots of town including the Locarno, the Market Place and Markeaton Park. On the day of the Animals concert we parked the car opposite the large queue waiting for the doors of the Gaumont to open. It had the desired effect and caused quite a stir. At that time Tommy looked a bit like Paul McCartney and the car was soon surrounded by a bevy of girls who were convinced that we were part of the Animals and that I was their lead singer, Eric Burden. Autograph books were thrust through the open window of the car and, of course, we gladly obliged. I often wonder how many counterfeit Eric Burden autographs there must be around Derby.

I was there!

7th November 1964
Barbara Zoppi (nee Cater)
Chaddesden, Derby

I couldn't get a ticket for this show so earlier that afternoon I hung around outside the stage door with my friend. A boy came out onto Osmaston Road and asked us where he could buy a tie. We didn't recognise him as being one of the stars of the

Stage door

show but it turned out to be Hilton Valentine, The Animals drummer. So we took him down St Peters Street to Burtons the Tailors. When we got back there was quite a crowd outside the stage door just waiting for someone famous to come out. Suddenly a Mini drove up and parked outside and out popped Eric Burden who made a dash for the stage doors. Everyone was screaming and thrusting autograph books in his direction but he didn't stop. So I nicked his petrol cap as a souvenir and when I got home I tried to make a necklace out of it but it didn't work.

Gerry & The Pacemakers

PROMOTERS: Brian Epstein/ Arthur Howes

GERRY & THE PACEMAKERS

GENE PITNEY

KINKS

MARIANNE FAITHFULL

MIKE COTTON SOUND

BOBBY SHAFTO

BRYAN BURDON (COMPÈRE)

No.1 ON THIS DAY

THE SUPREMES *Baby Love*

Liverpool group Gerry & The Pacemakers topped the bill of this Brian Epstein/ Arthur Howes show. They hit the big time immediately after the Beatles and were the first act to reach No.1 in the UK Singles Charts with their first three releases. Making more of a stir were new North London group The Kinks who got to top spot a couple of months earlier with their first hit *You Really Got Me*. Still managing to ride the wave of the British beat revolution was American star Gene Pitney who was making a return visit to Derby after supporting the all-star 'Mersey Beat' show earlier that year. His *I'm Gonna Be Strong* entered the Top 20 that day and would go on the reach No.2. Also in support was Marianne Faithfull whose first hit *As Tears Go By* had just left the charts. She shot to fame that year after attending a Rolling Stones party where she was discovered by their manger Andrew Loog Oldham. Also back stage that night was an unknown early American Motown artist Kim Weston although she didn't appear on the bill or pre-show publicity, nor was she mentioned in the show's reviews. However, that night she was due to appear in Hanley with the Earl Van Dyke Quartet on a postponed P J Proby package tour, so perhaps she just went along for the ride. She would later find chart success in 1967 singing duet with Marvin Gaye on *It Takes Two*.

GAUMONT • DERBY
Phone : 44744
Manager : H. BEDFORD
6.0 **SATURDAY, 21st NOVEMBER** 8.30
TWO PERFORMANCES ONLY

FOR ONE DAY ONLY **ON THE STAGE** FOR ONE DAY ONLY
(INSTEAD OF THE USUAL FILM PROGRAMME)

ARTHUR HOWES & BRIAN EPSTEIN present

GERRY AND THE **PACEMAKERS**

GENE PITNEY FROM THE U.S.A.

Marianne **FAITHFULL**

BOBBY SHAFTO WITH THE **ROOFRAISERS**

MIKE COTTON SOUND YOUR COMPÈRE **BRYAN BURDON**

THE DYNAMIC **KINKS**

PRICES : 10/6 8/6 6/6

Photo: Eric Chapman

I was there!

21st November 1964
Barbara Zoppi
(nee Cater)
Chaddesden, Derby

I had managed to get a front row ticket for this show and earlier that day quite a lot of fans had congregated around the Spot area of town. Marian Faithful was always in the papers around that time for various reasons and when she emerged from the front of the Gaumont she was mobbed by the crowd. Some 'minders' ushered her into Daltons radio, TV and record store across the road so that she could take refuge. We all tried to follow her in and I remember Miss Faithful turned to me and, in a very posh voice, said 'Oh, please don't push'. I don't remember much about her performance on stage that night but I do remember that the Kinks and Gene Pitney brought the house down. But for me Gerry and the Pacemakers were certainly the stars of that show.

Gene Pitney
Photo: Eric Chapman

The Kinks
Photo: Eric Chapman

I was there!

**21st November 1964
Pauline Sims
(nee Byard)
Swarkestone, Derby**

This was the second time that year that I had managed to persuade my boyfriend, Brian, to take me to see Gene Pitney at the Gaumont. I used to tell him that Gene Pitney made my socks revolve. He may have been a little jealous at the time but we did eventually marry in 1967 so Mr Pitney missed out. Anyway, Brian was quite happy to see The Kinks who had just had their first hit You Really Got Me and perhaps stole the show that night.

Marianne Faithfull
with Kim Weston
Photo: Eric Chapma

I was there!

21st November 1964
Gerry & The Pacemakers
Patrick Flood
Alvaston, Derby

In my capacity as Junior Doorman working the back stage area of the Gaumont I saw lots of things. But for me this show was by far the most eventful. The manager of the theatre, Harry Bedford, had previously had problems with artists taking girls back into their dressing rooms. So on this night he told me that on no circumstances was I to allow this to happen. I was patrolling back stage after one of the groups had just completed their performance and was confronted with the heavily perspiring group members in hunting jackets climbing the stairs to the dressing rooms with a girl tow. I was only a lad of 18 but I told them as forcefully as I could that the girl wasn't allowed any further. The group's leader wasn't having any of it and started arguing with me saying that she was a close friend. In the end the frightened girl ran back down the stairs and disappeared. The band members pushed passed me muttering obscenities before slamming their dressing room door behind them.

Very soon after that I heard what sounded like a physical argument taking place inside with furniture being thrown around and I'll never forget hearing the words "I told you what I'd f*****g do if you took my girl". The door suddenly opened and one of the guitarists backed out saying "No, no, don't do it" and he was followed by his brother pointing what looked like a starting pistol and shouting "I'm going to f*****g do it!" I was so petrified I froze on the spot until they both started rolling around laughing at me. It had been a send-up to get back for spoiling their fun. There is another event from that night that sticks in my mind. Later, during my behind-the-scenes patrol I stumbled across Gene Pitney in a passionate clinch with a girl singer who was also on the bill and whenever I hear his hit Back Stage on the radio I wonder if this liaison influenced his song.

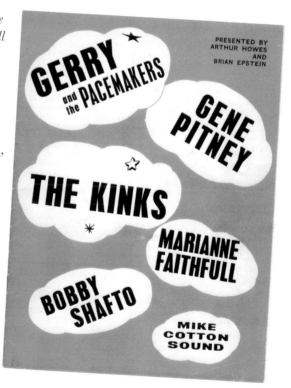

Chapter 7

1965
The beginning of the end as the shows dwindle

23rd May 1965

The Hollies and The Walker Brothers

PROMOTER:
Arthur Howes

WALKER BROTHERS

THE HOLLIES

GOLDIE & THE GINGERBREADS

JEFF & JON

RIOT SQUAD

VAL MCKENNA

BOB BAIN (COMPÈRE)

No.1 ON THIS DAY

JACKIE TRENT
Where Are You Now My Love

This show was originally promoted as being headlined by the Kinks and The Yardbirds but The Kinks left the show 4 days earlier after Dave Davies and drummer Mick Avory had a fight onstage at the Capitol Cinema, Cardiff with Davies needing hospital treatment. The Yardbirds also left the tour to fulfil prior bookings in Scotland and both headliners were replaced by the Walker Brothers and The Hollies for the final four dates including Derby. Before coming over from the USA for this British tour the Walker Brothers had notched-up a Top 20 hit with *Love Her* and would go on to hit the top spot three months later with *Make It Easy On Yourself*. Joint last minute headliners The Hollies entered the charts that week with their eighth release and first No.1 *I'm Alive*. Another act from the USA, Goldie & The Gingerbreads, were the first all-female rock band to be signed to a major record label. They joined the tour on the back of their only hit *Can't You Hear My Heart Beat* which made No.25 in the UK. The appearance of London band The Riot Squad included Graham Bonney in its line-up who, a year later and following three unsuccessful Joe Meek produced singles, left the band to enjoy a solo hit with *Super Girl*. The Riot Squad continued with various personnel changes which included David Bowie who sang with the group just before releasing his self-titled debut album in 1967. Also on the bill was 16-year-old Val McKenna who had just released her Carter/Lewis song *Baby Do It* but it failed to chart.

GAUMONT : Derby
STAGE SHOW
2nd Performance 8-30 p.m.
SUNDAY
MAY **23**
2
FRONT STALLS 10/6

C 7

No ticket exchanged nor money refunded
THIS PORTION TO BE RETAINED

I was here!

23rd May 1965
The Hollies and The Walker Brothers
Derby Evening Telegraph

A bit of a storm blew up at the Gaumont, Derby, last night when Liverpool group The Hollies arrived and found that they were not top of the bill. Top billing was given to The Walker Brothers, who it was announced on Friday, replaced the Kinks after they withdrew from the tour because of an incident on stage in Cardiff. The Hollies thought that they should have pride of place instead of The Walker Brothers, who are not so well known, "We've never heard of them", declared Tony Hicks, lead guitarist with the group". We don't mind the Hollies going on last," said John, one of the Walkers. We didn't think we would get top billing anyway."

3rd October 1965

Cliff Richard & The Shadows

CLIFF RICHARD & THE SHADOWS

This was the eighth appearance of the most popular act to ever visit the Gaumont Cinema in Derby. March that year saw the end of Cliff's amazing run of 23 consecutive Top 10 hits after *The Minute You're Gone* had made the top spot. His next two singles only managed No.12 and 22 respectively but this was a small blip in the stars stellar career and his *Wind Me Up* would make No.2 just a month after this performance. Nevertheless it was a sign of the times and the demise of the traditional lead-singer/guitar group line-up. This was underlined by the fact that The Shadows were struggling to maintain their popularity as a solo act. However, they still had a large band of loyal fans and their vocal *Don't Make My Baby Blue* had made No.10 five weeks earlier.

No.1 ON THIS DAY

KEN DODD
Tears

I was there!

**3rd October 1965
Barbara Jones
Derby Evening
Telegraph**

Meeting Cliff Richard for the first time between his appearances in the stage show at the Gaumont on Sunday night made a five-year-old Derby youngster's dream come true. Carried into Cliff's backstage dressing room, little Susan Hitchcock's face lit up into a great big smile, because, with both legs encased in plaster, life is anything but a bed of roses for young Susan these days. Susan, whose home is at 53 Burnsby Street, Crewton, Derby, is suffering from a disease of the hip. She is a frequent visitor to Derbyshire Children's Hospital, North Street, where she receives treatment for her complaint. Both her legs have been in plaster casts for 15 months now. Susan is a pupil at Wilmorton Infants' School and all her friends are envious of her meeting Cliff. Cliff made such a fuss of her, for he signed his autograph on her plaster cast and gave her a specially big kiss.

20th November 1965

The Marquee Show

Topping the bill were Manfred Mann and The Yardbirds and this was the first national package show to visit Derby's iconic venue after changing its name from The Gaumont to The Odeon. The tour was promoted as 'The Marquee Show' in deference to London's popular Blues and R&B Club which had influenced many British bands including the two headliners. Manfred Mann's fifth Top 10 hit *If You Gotta Go Go Now* had just left the charts and The Yardbirds double-sided single *Evil Hearted You/Still I'm Sad* was in the Top 10. Paul Jones was still lead singer with The Manfreds and The Yardbirds featured Jeff Beck on lead guitar after he had taken over from Eric Clapton earlier that year. Favourites with the female member of the audience that night were brothers Paul & Barry Ryan, the sons of 50s singer Marion Ryan, and they were charting that week with their debut hit *Don't Bring Me Your Heartaches*. Paul went solo three years later with his No.2 hit *Eloise*. Also on the bill were American R&B stars Inez & Charlie Foxx whose recording of *Mockingbird* was a cult favourite in the Mod all-nighter clubs that were now springing up around Britain. Completing the line-up were Gary Farr & The T-Bones, The Mark Leeman 5 and the then unknown Scaffold which included Paul McCartney's brother Mike McGear. The Folk-influenced Scaffold would eventually find fame with their novelty hit singles *Thank U Very Much* and *Lilly The Pink*.

No.1 ON THIS DAY
THE ROLLING STONES
Get Off Of My Cloud

PROMOTERS:
George Cooper Organisation
'The Marquee Show'

**MANFRED MANN
YARDBIRDS**

PAUL & BARRY RYAN

INEZ & CHARLIE FOXX

MARK LEEMAN 5

SCAFFOLD

GARY FARR & THE T-BONES

ODEON THEATRE - DERBY
STAGE SHOW
2nd Performance 8-30 p.m.
SATURDAY
NOVEMBER 20
FRONT STALLS 12/6
D 6
No ticket exchanged nor money refunded
THIS PORTION TO BE RETAINED

THE marquee SHOW

3972

Chapter 8

1966
A final flurry from Rock and Pop legends before the curtain came down

27th March 1966

Roy Orbison & Walker Brothers

PROMOTER: Arthur Howes

ROY ORBISON
WALKER BROTHERS
LULU & THE LUVVERS
THE MARIONETTES
KIM 'D' & THE DEL FIVE
THE QUOTATIONS
RAY CAMERON (COMPĒRE)

Although Roy Orbison and The Walker Brothers shared top billing for this show it could be argued that The Walker Brothers had eclipsed him in terms of popularity at this time. Since their last appearance in Derby 10 months earlier the American heart throbs had enjoyed a No.1 and No.3 respectively with *Make It Easy On Yourself* and *My Ship Is Coming In* and on this day their latest *The Sun Ain't Gonna Shine Anymore* was at the top of the UK charts. As for 'The Big O' he hadn't made the Top 20 since 1964 although with dozens of hits stretching back to 1960 he was still a box office draw and was already enjoying legendary status. In support were Lulu & The Luvvers. At only 15 years old the Scottish singer made her name a couple of years earlier with a cover of the Isley Brothers *Shout* which made No.7 in the charts. Despite not having much success with her follow-up singles up until her Derby appearance she would go on to have a highly successful career as a singer, TV personality, actress and model. Backing The Walkers was seven-piece British band The Quotations which included bass player Johnny 'Gus' Gustafson who would go on to become a member of Roxy Music in the early 70s. Also in support were a two girl/two boy vocal quartet The Marionettes and Newcastle born Kim 'D' with her backing group the Del Five. Making a return to Derby as compère was Canadian comedian Ray Cameron - the father of TV stand-up star Michael McIntyre.

No.1 ON THIS DAY
THE WALKER BROTHERS
The Sun Ain't Gonna Shine Anymore

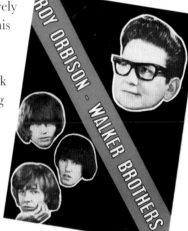

27th March 1966
Lucy Orgill
Littleover, Derby

In the late 50s and early 60s, I was a regular at the Gaumont, where I interviewed Cliff Richard, twice I think, The Kinks, The Hollies, and once bumped into a glamorous Dusty Springfield, with her brothers, before she became a solo artist and an icon. I was working, until 1960, for The Derbyshire Times in Chesterfield, and after that, was asked to do 'snippets' for the New Musical Express (or it could have been the Melody Maker - memories play tricks at my age!) which meant hanging around, doing the odd interview and picking up odd bits of gossip. My interview with the Walker Brothers on the night, while my boy-friend, now husband, John met Roy Orbison, didn't go too well. Indeed, it was a disaster, with Scott being especially reticent and other members showing signs of boredom. Okay, they were downright rude, so it was a disappointment. But in more than 50 years in journalism, it was a one-off, so I've not dwelt on it. I actually revelled in the atmosphere back-stage, with screaming, crying fans outside, the ubiquitous 'stage door manager' storming around trying to keep order, and the adrenalin rush as the dressing room door opened and we scribes were ushered into the inner sanctum. Heady, happy days!

27th March 1966
John Orgill
Littleover, Derby

When Roy Orbison died in 1988 it sent me off into "boring my friends reminiscing mode". I had interviewed him for the Derby Evening Telegraph in March 1966 when he appeared in concert at the Odeon, Derby. My news editor had assigned me to try to get back stage after the concert and have a chat with Roy, who was then - and still is - one of my favourite artists. I turned up outside his dressing room and checked with his manager that I could ask Roy about his relationship with his wife Claudette whom he divorced and had recently re-married. No problem. It was supposed to be a reporter/star interview, but turned out to be a pleasant chat. He smoked French cigarettes and he offered me one which I accepted. And he didn't seem particularly eager to terminate the interview as soon as possible. We soon realised we had something in common - motor-cycles. He rode the great Harley-Davison, but I had to make do with a more modest 500cc Matchless machine. In fact during this UK tour, Roy could not resist when he was offered a spin on a motor-cycle round a race track. Unfortunately he fell off and broke his foot. But he carried on with the concert. No wonder he didn't move around much! His performance before I met him that evening was brilliant. So it was with tragic irony that his recently re-married wife Claudette was killed in a motor cycle accident just a few months after my interview.

I was there!

27th March 1966
Barbara Zoppi (nee Cater)
Chaddesden

My friend, Ruth, and I really fancied the Walker Brothers, especially Scott Walker, and we managed to get seats just behind the front row so that we could get a close look at them. Seeing Roy Orbison also sticks in my mind because he was dressed in all black except that one of his legs was in a white plaster cast which he supported on a stool while he performed. I later learned that he had visited the Derbyshire Royal Infirmary before the show and had his leg dressed by my best friend's mother who was a nurse at the hospital. After the show we hung around outside the front entrance in the hope of meeting the Walker Brothers. After quite a while our patience paid off and out they came, but Ruth ran up to John Walker shouting Scott! Scott! which was very embarrassing. This was one of the last shows I saw at the Gaumont but I still travel the country to see concerts and I often visit the Flowerpot in King Street, Derby.

Roy Orbison
Photo: Eric Chapman

The Who and The Spencer Davis Group

This tour, which had taken the whole country by storm and is still talked about today, could have been called 'The Battle of Britain's New Bands' with two of the most successful groups of the time sharing top billing. The Who were still in the charts with their third Top 10 hit *Substitute* while The Spencer Davis Group had just enjoyed their second No.1 *Somebody Help Me*, their follow-up to *Keep On Running*. This wasn't the first time that the members of The Who performed in Derby. They appeared at the Corporation Hotel near the old Cattle Market in May 1964 under the name The High Numbers. The rest of the show's line-up makes interesting reading with the relatively unknown Jamaican-born ska and reggae musician Jimmy Cliff much lower down on the bill. He had been spotted in New York by Spencer Davis manager, Chris Blackwell, who persuaded him to try his luck in the UK. However, Jimmy Cliff had to wait until late 1969 before finding chart success with *Wonderful World, Beautiful People*. Also appearing were Liverpool duo and ex-Merseybeat members Tony Crane and Billy Kinsley under the name The Merseys. Their first and only hit, a cover of USA group The McCoys *Sorrow*, entered the charts during the week of this show and went on to reach No.4. In support were The Fruit Eating Bears, Hamilton, Paul Dean & The Soul Savages and Mike Sarne who was making a return to Derby having appeared on the Billy Fury show in October 1962.

No.1 ON THIS DAY

THE WALKER BROTHERS
The Sun Ain't Gonna Shine Anymore

PROMOTER: Robert Stigwood

THE WHO
THE SPENCER DAVIS GROUP

THE FABULOUS NEW MERSEYS

THE FRUIT EATING BEARS

MIKE SARNE

BAND OF ANGELS

JIMMY CLIFF AND THE SOUND SYSTEM

HAMILTON

PAUL DEAN & THE SOUL SAVAGES

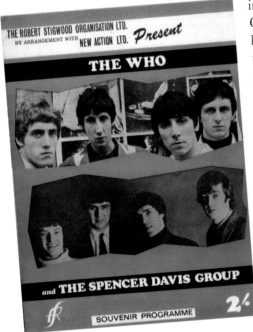

THE ROBERT STIGWOOD ORGANISATION LTD. BY ARRANGEMENT WITH NEW ACTION LTD. *Present*

THE WHO

and THE SPENCER DAVIS GROUP

SOUVENIR PROGRAMME   2/-

I was there!

22nd April 1966
Alan Atkin
The Square & Compass
Darley Dale, Derbyshire

As a school boy growing up in the Derbyshire Dales I always felt a world away from the 'Swinging Sixties' but for some reason I took an early interest in pop music. I may have been influenced by my Aunty Lucy who, as a young journalist with the Derbyshire Times, was in touch with modern trends in fashion and music. To me she achieved legendary status when she told me that, after interviewing Billy Fury following his appearance at The Ritz cinema in Matlock, the star walked her home all the way to Darley Bridge, some two miles away. She later became one of the most popular writers on the Derby Evening Telegraph under her married name, Lucy Orgill. My early rock'n'roll favourites were Elvis and Cliff but at the age of 13 when the British beat groups took over the pop scene my tastes changed. I couldn't believe it when Aunty got me a ticket to see The Who and Spencer Davis in Derby. I travelled from Matlock on the train and was met by Aunty Lucy and her friend Philippa Henderson. But to my surprise they just gave me my ticket and dumped me outside saying that they were off round town and would pick me up outside the Gaumont afterwards (I'm sure it would have been different had Billy Fury been on that night). So I bought myself a programme in the cinema foyer which seemed so big and grand and made my way to my seat on the balcony. I watched the show sitting by myself but was totally absorbed by the performers, especially The Who. I also remember the reggae songs from, a then unknown, Jimmy Cliff which was a style of music I'd never heard before. The next day my souvenir programme was the talk of the playground at Lady Manners School in Bakewell.

ODEON THEATRE - DERBY
THE WHO
2nd Performance at 8-40 p.m.
FRIDAY
APRIL **22**
FRONT STALLS 12/6

F 6
No ticket exchanged nor money refunded
THIS PORTION TO BE RETAINED

22nd April 1966
Eric Chapman
Stapleford, Nottingham

At one of the last Gaumont shows I had the opportunity to photograph The Who. I knocked on their dressing room door which was opened by Roger Daltry. When I explained why I was there he invited me in and asked me to wait while he got ready. He disappeared into a side room and was gone for quite a while. I tried to talk to Pete Townshend but he seemed totally disinterested and as if he was on another planet. Eventually Daltry returned from his tittifications and said that he was ready. Well, in those days of film and processing, the newspaper wasn't prepared to reimburse me for my materials so I just took a couple of shots. But Roger Daltry wasn't impressed and said something like "Is that it? I've just spent 15 minutes doing my hair". With my last few frames of film I managed to capture The Spencer Davis Group with Stevie Winwood. The old camera I used only took films with 12 exposures and I had just one film with me - how I regret it. But nevertheless, when the show started, I stood in the wings and along with the vast audience really enjoyed that show.

16th September 1966

The Who

PROMOTER: Robert Stigwood

THE WHO

THE FANTASTIC
NEW MERSEYS

THE FRUIT EATING BEARS

OSCAR

THE MAGIC LANTERNS

THE MI FIVE

SPECIAL GUEST STAR:
MAX WALL

The Who made a speedy return to Derby having headlined with The Spencer Davis Group just five months earlier. They were quickly establishing themselves internationally although they had to wait until the following year before they broke into the USA. On the day of this concert *I'm A Boy* was in the Top 20 and would go on to reach No.2. Around the same time *The Kids Are Alright* was released by the band's original record company, Brunswick, and it made a brief appearance in the charts at No.41 earlier that month. With the Who's meteoric rise in popularity, their return concert sold-out much quicker than their earlier visit. Also returning after the April concert were The Merseys and The Fruit Eating Bears along with a rather bizarre special guest star - the 50s TV comedian/actor Max Wall who was famous for his black tights and silly walk. Completing the bill were The Magic Lanterns, The MI Five and Oscar.

No.1
ON THIS DAY
THE BEATLES
Yellow Submarine/
Eleanor Rigby

I was there!

16th September 1966
Margaret Adams
Derby

I witnessed both performances by The Who when I was just 15. The day the tickets went on sale my father sent his apprentice to the box office at 7.30am to get my friend and I front row seats. That accomplished, our next task was to get the afternoon off school. We both forged letters to our teachers saying we had dental appointments and then went down on the bus to join the other fans around the Gaumont (then renamed the Odeon) to wait for the groups to arrive. We had written to the fan club, of which we were members, to get a letter to go backstage. The previous week, we went to the manager of the Gaumont with said letter but he was having none of it. On the afternoon of the gig, we showed the letter to the assistant manager, who organised for us to go backstage after the first show and meet our idols. We could not believe our luck.

I was there!

16th September 1966
Barbara Zoppi (nee Cater)
Chaddesden, Derby

I was in pole position to see The Who, having managed to get front row tickets by going early. I lived on a farm which was well out of town and I cycled to my friend's house to get the workman's bus to sit on the very cold steps of the Gaumont to wait for the ticket office to open. If we didn't get the front row we didn't want to go and we were first in the queue as usual when it opened at 9am. We paid very little for the tickets, no more than five bob (25p), possibly less. I wish I'd kept the ticket. They were loud, loud, loud! To be honest, I can remember more about meeting Pete Townshend afterwards than I can the actual show but I think The Who are the best group we've ever seen in this country.

The Who
Photo: Eric Chapman

87

23rd October 1966

The Walker Brothers Show

PROMOTER: Arthur Howes

WALKER BROTHERS

THE TROGGS

DAVE DEE, DOZY, BEAKY, MICK & TICH

CLODA ROGERS

THE MONTANAS

THE QUOTATIONS

DON CROCKETT (COMPÈRE)

This was the last of the large pop package tours to visit Derby's Gaumont cinema, then called the Odeon. The event was promoted as The Walker Brothers Show on the back of their short but spectacular UK chart success which included two chart toppers and a No.2 in just over 6 months. The American trio had headlined at their previous Derby show earlier that year while *The Sun Ain't Gonna Shine Anymore* was at the top of the charts. Unfortunately their next two releases failed to make the Top 20 and soon after this tour The Walker Brothers disbanded although Scott did find solo success in the late 60s. However, the two main support acts were fairing much better in the charts at that time. The Troggs *Can't Control Myself* was at No.4 and would go on to reach No.2 while Dave Dee, Dozy, Beaky, Mick & Tich were at No.3 with *Bend It*. Also in support was a then unknown Clodagh Rodgers

No.1 ON THIS DAY
JIM REEVES
Distant Drums

who would have to wait until March 1969 to have her first hit *Come Back And Shake Me* which would get to No.3. The Walker Brothers seven-piece backing band The Quotations were making a return visit to Derby and the show was opened by Wolverhampton group The Montanas. As the curtain came down on the Walker Brothers it brought to an end a magical seven year period during which over two hundred national and international hit makers graced the stage of this iconic Derby theatre.

Arthur Howes presents
The WALKER BROTHERS show

23rd October 1966
Rod Lyons
The Derbyshire Advertiser

Derby Odeon was sold out for both houses of the Walker Brothers Show, on Sunday night, and all the performers received a tremendous and noisy reception from Derby's teenagers.

Appearing with the Walker Brothers were Dave Dee, Dozy, Beaky, Mick and Tich, The Troggs and The Quotations (the Walkers backing group), who all received a screaming ovation from the audience. The Troggs gave the best performance of the evening in my opinion, and this was born out by the reception they were given by the audience. Their performance was sensational and apart from singing the numbers which made them famous, they did an exceptionally good rendering of the number off the Stones first L.P. entitled Mona. In an interview with Pete Staples of The Troggs, he said that he thought the Derby audience were "great."

The Walkers Brothers
Photo: Eric Chapman

Derby's 'super cinema' the Gaumont Palace opened in 1934. The monumental Art Deco style building had a flight of white stone steps leading from street level to an impressive marble floored and walnut panelled foyer. The auditorium was dominated by an imposing decorative ceiling and the Gaumont Palace quickly established itself as Derby's leading cinema.

As cinema audiences began to dwindle in the late fifties and at the start of the new decade other Derby cinemas began to close. But the Gaumont boosted takings by becoming the local venue for the Pop Package Tour concerts which were touring Britain.

In 1965, when the Rank Organisation closed the nearby Odeon Cinema on St. Peter Street, the Gaumont was renamed the Odeon. By this time the package tours had almost had their day although the cinema did continue to stage the odd pop concert until the end of the decade.

The iconic Derby theatre continued to limp along as a cinema and the building was altered in 1974 with a drop wall from the balcony front creating two mini-cinemas. Despite the shiny new refit and being renamed The Odeon the venue was still popularly referred to as The Gaumont for years to come.

On 3rd of May 1983 The Odeon cinema closed its door after its final showing of Gandhi. Cinema manager Graham Dilks marked the event by donning a pristine dinner suit to welcome his final guests as they made their way up the steps to the cinema entrance.

ABC purchased the cinema and re-launched it as the ABC Trocadero Entertainment Centre. The expensive structural conversion split the building horizontally to form a single screen cinema and a bingo hall. Sadly, most of its original Art Deco style interior features were lost.

The cinema was called the ABC Trocadero Entertainment Centre. This left Derby with just one commercial cinema screen which was very frustrating as there was little film choice. The cinema changed its name one final time when it became the Cannon.

Then in 1988 Derby received two ten-screen mutiplex cinemas on opposite sides of the city.

The Cannon was set to struggle on, then one morning shortly before the cinema opened for the kids club, the ornate plaster ceiling collapsed, wrecking the auditorium. The final film to play was Sean Penn in 'Willow' on 17th December 1988.

The cinema never reopened and lay empty for many years until the bingo moved out too leaving only a dance school operating in the former café on the top floor.

Then, just after the turn of the century, the auditorium was gutted and the entire building was converted into a nightclub and banqueting centre called Zanzibar which closed after a decade in January 2010. The building lay empty until the spring of 2013 when it was converted into a buffet-style restaurant.

While this iconic building still stands today and operates as the Cosmo restaurant it will always be remembered for its more glamorous days when artists such as Cliff Richard, Little Richard, Roy Orbison, The Rolling Stones, The Who and The Kinks graced its stage.

The old stage door on Osmaston Road at the rear of the Gaumont

Roger Smith has music running through his veins. At the 'birth' of British pop in the early 60s he was playing bass guitar in Derby semi-pro groups The Rapids and Godfreys Grit'n'Soul Band. By the middle of the 'Swinging Sixties' he temporarily hung up his Fender bass and spent his spare-time helping to establish Derby's Soul scene with Discovery Discotheque, Clouds (later Cleopatra's) and Shotgun Discotheque.

Roger worked at The Derbyshire Advertiser and The Derby Evening Telegraph for many years and in 1975 joined Derby County Football Club, then Football League Champions, as Advertising and Sponsorship Executive. He formed Smith East Associates in 1977, with Trevor East, which became one of the region's leading advertising agencies. He has lived in Derby all his life and is still working as a marketing consultant, but he still finds time to thump out 60s rock'n'roll, soul and pop with Godfreys Grit'n'Soul Band, just as he did more than 50 years ago.

The Gaumont pop concerts encapsulated an era of great music and great musicians which formed the bedrock of Derby's growing music scene. And Roger Smith was part of it all in those exciting, heady times.

By Richard Cox, a member of the renowned Derby Evening Telegraph 'Saturday Page' crew from 1970 to 1977.

The Photographer

The majority of the photographs in this book were taken by my dear friend Eric Chapman and it was these fascinating shots that inspired me to write this book.

Eric was born in Derby in 1932 and worked as a compositor for the Derbyshire Advertiser from 1947 until 1969. In his spare time Eric was an amateur photographer and keen bodybuilder and he soon became one of the leading contributors to the international body-building press. His early photographs of Derby's World champion weight-lifter, Louis Martin, appeared in publications throughout the globe.

When the pop package tours came to Derby in the early 60s, the editor of the Derbyshire Advertiser asked Eric if he would support the staff photographer and cover the events in his spare time. Eric was a keen music fan, although the Latin American sounds of the day were his real passion, and so, after encouragement from me, Eric agreed. This started an adventure that, little known to Eric, would capture the evidence that many future international artists had once graced the stage of Derby's Gaumont cinema.

I believe that Eric's secret was in the natural warmth which he always exuded, even when meeting the rich and famous, and I am sure this helped put his subjects at ease. His work captures a rare, candid glimpse of the pop stars of the 60s compared with the results of their over-produced studio promotional shots.

Roger Smith

Thanks

The author would like to thank the following for their help with this book.

Eric Chapman: All the Photographs taken in the dressing rooms of the Gaumont Cinema, Derby

David Foster: Design collaboration and artwork

Ian Morley, Wirksworth, Derbyshire: Memorabilia

Peter Brown, Mickleover, Derby: Help with local newspaper research

Dan Wheeler, The Photo Parlour, Nottingham: Photo restoration

Bob Allen Photos, Allenton, Derby: Photo restoration

Woody, Cinema Treasures: Gaumont History

Thanks also for the help, advice and encouragement received from the following:

Dave Berry, John Colley, Richard Cox, Lynne Dixon, Mike Foster, Jane Goddard (Derby Telegraph), Richard Houghton (Gotta Have Books), Lucy and John Orgill, Anton Rippon, Sara Smith and of course, all the 'I Was There' contributors. Finally a big bouquet to my dear wife Maria for putting up with two years of my periodic, virtual absence.

Framed Photographs

All the photographs taken by Eric Chapman in this book are available framed. The 10″ x 8″ hand-made, silver gelatine pints are available with or without mounts in a a variety of frame sizes.

For a full price list please contact thephotoparlour@gmail.com
www.photo-parlour.com

Another title by the author – Available 2018

Rum'n'Coke, a fiction novel written by Roger Smith, will be available early 2018. The book is set in a provincial town in the early 1960s and highlights the important issues in the lives of most young people – work and play, love and sex, fashion and music, fear and danger. It's a sort of modern picaresque novel, tracing the rites of passage through which the teenage hero's life takes him. The book features an original device for the sub-sections of each chapter. It uses pop song titles from the time in which it is set, each one loosely relating to the

developing narrative. The chapter titles then reflect stages in the hero's life and adventures. Besides the humorous, intriguing and mysterious storyline the book presents a valuable insight into the social history from the period.

For more information please contact enquiries@thetap-publishing.com